EDNA HIBEL:
Her Life and Art

Written by
Olga Cossi

With art by
Edna Hibel

Discovery Enterprises, Ltd.
Lowell, Massachusetts
1994

© Olga Cossi, text; Edna Hibel, artwork 1994

Library edition ISBN 1-878668-31-5

Library of Congress Catalog Card Number 94-70009

10   9   8   7   6   5   4   3   2   1

Printed in the United States of America

A Word on the Literature

Much of the story of Edna Hibel's life found in this book is based upon personal interviews with Edna and her family conducted by the author, Olga Cossi, and by the editor, JoAnne B. Weisman. Other valuable sources include *Edna Hibel, an album and biography*, by Kay Pedrick, copyright 1985 Tradition Ink; and the many newsletters of the Edna Hibel Society, written and published by Ralph Burg.

Subject Reference Guide

Cossi, Olga
Edna Hibel: Her Life and Art

1. Hibel, Edna – Biography
2. Artists – American
3. Women – American Artists

Special Acknowledgment

Many thanks to Tod Plotkin, Edna's husband, and to Dr. Andy Plotkin, Executive Trustee of the Hibel Museum of Art, and middle son, for their endless hours of searching for photos and documenting Edna's life to allow this book to come together.

Special acknowledgment from the Publisher goes to Ralph Burg, as well, who not only shared many Hibel anecdotes and newsletter stories with us, but also has worked to introduce Edna Hibel's art to thousands of people all over the world.

Dedication

To my sisters, Anne and Rina,
who share my appreciation of Edna Hibel,
the woman and the artist.

— Olga Cossi

Edna Hibel

What a blessing it has been to be an artist. It is such a thrill to see my ideas take shape, grow, and mature as I search for beauty and meaning in the colors, lines, forms, and their dynamics.

How else could I ever express my deepest feelings about humanity and this miraculous world.

— Edna Hibel

First Signs of Talent

The first hint that Edna Hibel had artistic talent surfaced when she was in the fourth grade at the Andrew Jackson School in Allston, Massachusetts. School work was very easy for Edna, especially arithmetic. She finished her assignments quickly, and was always eager for another challenge.

"What should I do now?" she would ask her teacher.

The teacher did her best to keep Edna busy. One day when she could think of nothing else to give the young girl to do, she handed Edna a box of watercolors and a brush and told her to paint a picture. She also gave her a copy of *Good Housekeeping Magazine* and suggested she copy the illustration on the cover.

Edna had never tried painting or drawing before. The only artwork she had ever done was in coloring books. She liked coloring with crayons and was always very careful to stay within the lines of the pictures.

That day in the classroom, Edna picked up the paintbrush and looked at the row of watercolors given to her. Here was a strangely intriguing challenge. As she began to copy the picture on the magazine cover, something magical seemed to happen to the brush in her fingers. The picture flowed on the paper quickly and easily. Before long the picture was finished and ready to turn in.

The teacher was impressed. Even though the drawing was only a copy, she could see that it was well done and had an artistic charm not present in the original. She hung the picture on the wall in the classroom. She did not know it, but she was exhibiting Edna Hibel's first painting. Today

Proud parents, Lena and Abraham, with Edna at two months. Edna was born on January 13, 1917.

that childhood watercolor is displayed in the Hibel Museum of Art in Palm Beach, Florida. It is not for sale at any price.

When school was over that day, Edna brought home her little painting copied from the cover of *Good Housekeeping Magazine* and gave it to her mother, Lena Hibel. Mrs. Hibel was so impressed she went right out and bought her young daughter a frame for the picture and a full set of paints and brushes. She had no doubts about Edna's hidden talent. She was convinced that Edna could create original works of art that would some day win national and international honors.

Art came easily to Edna, just as her school work did. She enjoyed turning out one painting after another. She liked doing original sketches and she loved the pleasure they seemed to give everyone who saw them.

For several years, Lena Hibel continued buying art supplies for her daughter and Edna kept on drawing and painting, giving away each picture as soon as it was finished. She never imagined that what she was doing for fun would some day

6

turn into her life's work. She was too busy growing up, going to school and making friends to think of a future career. And, she was too busy dancing.

Dancing was the biggest thing in Edna's young life long before she started painting. There was always music of some sort around the house, from the piano which Edna played, or a violin, a fiddle, or the phonograph which the family enjoyed so much. Often friends came over to play their instruments or to listen and dance to the music.

Edna learned to dance almost as soon as she learned to walk. If there was no other music around, she would dance to the tune on her Swiss music box. She was barely three years old when her mother decided she was ready for lessons.

"Would you like to be a dancer?" Lena Hibel asked her daughter as she flitted around the living room keeping time with the lively tunes her father, Abraham, played on the phonograph.

Edna's painting of the Good Housekeeping Magazine *cover*

Dancing class, with Edna on the far left

Edna was so excited, she danced around the room one more time. "Yes!" she cried eagerly.

"Then you will have lessons," Lena Hibel promised. Abraham smiled and nodded his approval.

Edna was enrolled immediately in a class for three-year-olds and soon delighted her parents with the new steps she learned each week. She threw herself into the dancing lessons, becoming a capable and eager performer.

Even at an early age, Edna loved people and liked making them happy. She was also full of energy, so it came as no surprise that she favored acrobatic dancing. She would twist and bend her chubby body into all sorts of positions to bring smiles to the faces of whoever happened to be in the living room watching. She worked hard to perfect the dance steps and movements so she would be ready to entertain whenever she had a chance.

8

Edna was five years old when her younger brother Billy was born. His arrival was the most wonderful thing that had ever happened. She adored the baby and became his "other mother." As soon as he was big enough, she played outdoors with Billy and his friends and became "one of the boys."

From the beginning, her relationship with Billy was one of completion, not competition. There was always love and affection for everyone in the Hibel family. Lena and Abraham did everything they could for both of their children. Her parents' attention did not seem to spoil Edna, but rather gave her an example to follow. She grew up to be as loving and giving as they were.

"When you are only a kid brother, it's pretty special to be allowed to be part of your big sister's circle of friends," says Billy. "She included me in everything they did, even

Edna at three

the music and singing, and I was a living example of someone who couldn't carry a tune in a bucket. I thought she was something else. I still do."

By the time Edna was ten, a new interest came into her life, outdoor sports. She still used her expressive hands as part of her dance routines, but now those fingers were just as good at catching and throwing a baseball, swinging a bat, handling a tennis racquet, or fishing.

Edna and her father shared a passion for fishing. From ages eleven through seventeen, Edna was Abraham's eager companion on fishing trips to Lake Mashpee on Cape Cod. They would rent a tiny cabin for the weekend and spend their time fishing, cooking out and exploring nature. Toward the end of those years at the cabin, Edna brought her watercolors with her and painted portraits of the Indian children at the lake. Recently one of those watercolors, "Mashpee Indian Boy," was donated to the Hibel Museum of Art and is now a treasured example of her early work.

There was only one thing Edna enjoyed doing with her father more than fishing. It was playing tennis. That game came close to becoming a career sport for Edna.

In those days, tennis was not the popular sport it is today. Still, it was a game Edna and her father enjoyed and learned to play together. Abraham and his daughter spent hours on the courts, with or without a net, banging away at balls. Edna's racquet wasn't much more than a toy, but she played with all her heart and made the best of it. They were having so much fun that Abraham did not think of buying his daughter a better racquet or seeing that she had professional lessons. Neither of them knew about such things. They enjoyed the game too much to take it seriously or think of tennis as a potential career.

In spite of her complete dedication to painting, Edna did go on to win several tennis trophies during her high school days as captain of the tennis team. Tennis has remained a hobby throughout her life, and she has passed the game on to her three grateful sons.

Tennis soon became one of the priorities in Edna's life. She was on the courts as often as she had the chance, especially when Abraham Hibel challenged his daughter to a game. There was hardly a day when the two of them were not rivals on the court. Nevertheless, Edna was still relatively untrained in the sport. She learned this the hard way when, at the age of fourteen, she entered her first school tournament.

Edna did very well in the play-offs. When she reached the finals, however, she faced a girl who had been competing in tournaments for years and was well on her way up the professional ladder. She defeated Edna quickly and easily.

That defeat was the turning point in Edna's tennis game. She had to decide either to get a good racquet and take lessons or continue to play just for the fun of it.

The choice was not a difficult one. By the age of fourteen, Edna had become so involved in her art that there was no time to pursue both interests. She was no longer merely dabbling at her easel or copying other people's drawings; she was creating original work, responding to the images that raced through her mind and painting anything that caught her eye. Art became the central focus in Edna's life.

Formal Art Training Begins

Shortly after Edna's twelfth birthday, she took her first important step toward a career in art. She joined a group of artists learning to draw the human figure by studying and sketching live models. An Italian couple who recognized artistic promise had seen Edna's paintings and felt she was mature enough to work with live nude models in order to understand the structure of the human form. They told her about night classes being held in Boston where a group of artists used nudes as their subjects. The couple encouraged Edna to enroll without delay and explained the value of such classes to her parents.

Edna immediately joined the group. Although the other students were at least twice her age, she was not self-conscious about her youth or about the models. She wanted to become a professional artist more than anything else. Edna never missed a class, concentrating on the subjects with the same incisive eye she was developing for whatever she drew or painted. She had seen the human body before and could accept it without embarrassment, clothed or unclothed, just as long as it gave her a chance to practice drawing.

At this early stage of her training, Edna was painting for the love of it. There were days when Edna would sit at her easel and work steadily for hours without stopping. On such days she would turn out as many as ten completed paintings. These she gave away as quickly as she could find someone to give them to. At other times, she would spend hours fussing over a small detail that she didn't think was quite good enough or didn't express exactly the image she had in mind. Sometimes

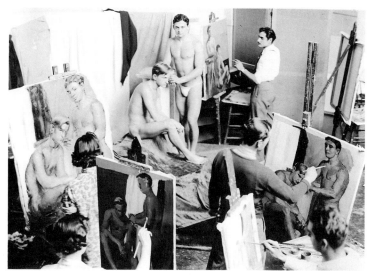

The young artist is in the middle, on the left.

she would work on such a detail for several days. Not a single painting was given away until it was, in her view, the very best she could do.

A year after Edna enrolled in the night classes, her formal art education began. She was thirteen and a freshman at Brookline High School.

Lena Hibel had taken one of Edna's paintings to the local frame shop to be framed so she could hang it in their home. While she was there, Gregory Michael, a noted Greek portrait painter, came in and saw the canvas she was holding. He studied the painting for a while, then asked about the artist who did it.

"My daughter, Edna, is the artist," Mrs. Hibel told him. "She is thirteen years old."

The art teacher was so impressed with the quality of the work of someone so young that he offered to take Edna as a student without charge. Lena thanked him for the offer, but insisted that she and Abraham pay for the lessons.

13

Every day after school Edna went to Gregory Michael's studio for a private session. Often on weekends she would be back for more lessons or to ask for help and advice about a particular painting she was working on.

Gregory Michael was a thorough teacher of the basic skills of art. He was patient with Edna and willing to allow her to find her own style and learn to perfect it. Edna had always "felt" whatever she tried to portray on paper or canvas. It was natural for her to rely on these feelings to decide what she wanted to bring out in each painting before she started her preliminary sketch. Now she was being taught how to express her feelings through her art in a professional way. She was learning to control her creative talent so she could accomplish what she set out to do. She was developing the skills of self-expression much like a child who has much to say and, word-by-word, learns to talk.

Under Gregory Michael's careful guidance, Edna's self-confidence grew line-by-line, sketch-by-sketch. She began trying

Painting in her attic at home. Age fifteen

Gregory Michael at work

new mediums and new ways of looking at things, always striving to improve herself. Even before she had a teacher, Edna was self-disciplined. Now that discipline became stronger than ever.

During the four years Edna was in high school, she continued her daily lessons with Gregory Michael. Despite that, she didn't give up any of her other activities such as tennis, basketball, or spending time with friends. Everything she did was met with the same enthusiasm and excitement as her painting.

On to Boston

E dna was only seventeen when she graduated from high school and immediately enrolled in the Boston Museum School of Fine Arts, one of the most respected art schools in the United States. While Edna was a student there, the school's three-year program was expanded to a five-year course.

Again, the young artist found that her assigned work came easily. In three months she completed the courses which normally took three years. She progressed from beginner to intermediate, then to advanced-level classes in a few weeks.

In the advanced group, Edna worked and studied alongside young adults with considerably more experience and background acquired in previous art schools they had attended. Most of them were much older than she, a fact she had learned to live with before.

They came to Boston primarily to work under one particular teacher on the staff, Alexander Yacovlev. Everyone was fascinated with him, both as a personality and as an outstanding instructor. Edna soon became one of his many followers.

Alexander Yacovlev was Russian by birth. He accepted the assignment to teach at the Boston Museum School of Fine Arts the year Edna enrolled. He was an exceptional and successful artist. He was also an exciting teacher and a popular one. Twice a week he critiqued each student's work. It wasn't long before Yacovlev noticed Edna's rare talent and youth.

One day while class was in session, Yacovlev stood behind Edna watching her work. That was not unusual. She was

Yacovlev hams it up at the beach.

Edna working on a fresco for school.

used to having her fellow students watch her at the easel. Yacovlev stood there quietly for a while before he spoke.

"You are a wunderkind!" he said, meaning a wonder child or genius.

Edna glowed with pride. "Coming from the great Alexander Yacovlev, that comment went right to my head," she recalls with a smile. "I felt six feet taller. But then, pride goes before a fall, doesn't it? Yacovlev was wise enough to see to it that I fell good and hard."

"You have a lot of talent," the teacher told the surprised girl, "but you must remember that it could mean nothing more than a lot of trouble for a young artist like you. When everything comes too easily and too quickly, that is not good. Talent needs to be perfected by effort, by hard work, or it will not bear lasting fruit."

His words left Edna feeling uneasy and deflated. "What

can I do?" she asked. She could not help it if she was a quick learner. It had always been that way, no matter what she tried.

"I will show you what to do," Yacovlev promised. "I will prescribe a special program for you, one you will not like, although later you will appreciate the results it is sure to bring for years to come."

The first thing the great teacher did was to make Edna change from drawing with a conte crayon, which was her favorite medium, to using a light grey crayon. With the conte, her strokes were bold and the effects were quick and flashy. This dramatic medium helped draw attention to her work with the least amount of effort. Naturally, the young artist liked that.

The grey crayon Yacovlev gave her was so light it hardly showed up on the paper. It took hours of practice and patience to get results. This meant that Edna had to master the execution of details, to command the art of draftsmanship or drawing. She lost her usual audience of admirers, who soon got tired of waiting around for her to get through all the little details. Instead, she gained valuable and needed training. Her fingers ached from the discipline required by the grey crayon, but gradually the control and skill came.

Those years studying in Boston were the most influential in Edna's development as an artist. Yacovlev was tireless as a teacher and watched over her progress with intense interest. He insisted that she continue to stretch her talent and her grasp of the techniques he taught in class. He was very strict with Edna, but he was just as careful to encourage her so she would stay with her studies.

To achieve the results he was after, Yacovlev made Edna practice drawing and painting still lifes. These are drawings or paintings of a single object or a few things artistically arranged in front of a plain background. The young artist found this work tedious, particularly when the medium she was now forced to use meant such slow, careful progress.

Once Yacovlev assigned Edna a still life of a stuffed bird. Drawing that bird was the most monotonous thing she had ever done. Each tiny feather had to be executed, line-by-line. She managed to make herself stay with it, although it seemed to take forever.

Yacovlev watched Edna struggle but made no comment. After a few minutes, he walked off, still without saying a word.

Half an hour later, Yacovlev returned from his apartment with a pair of worn pink ballet slippers. Yacovlev handed them to Edna and suggested she use them in the still life with the stuffed bird. The ballet slippers were signed inside, "To Sacha [a diminutive of Alexander] with love from Anna Pavlova," the great ballerina, who was rumored to have been in love with Yacovlev.

Edna was touched and impressed with the slippers, and Yacovlev's thoughtfulness in getting them for her. Their soft, simple lines and their delicate folds and creases offered a stark contrast to the fussy and complex details of the feathers. It was as if the teacher were giving her a lesson in the value of contrasts and at the same time rewarding the self-discipline she had shown when the work at hand was not to her liking.

Yacovlev's combination of strict supervision and wise encouragement was the best thing that could have happened to the budding artist. While Edna's hands were mastering the tools of her trade, her mind stretched to feel the reality and capture the spirit of her subject. Her studies taught her to sense the form, line, and color of the images she saw, then to grasp their meaning and embody it in her work.

Her training at the Boston school was just the beginning of what would take Edna years to achieve, but she was on her way.

First Sales

One measure of the success of an artist depends at least in part on the sale of what he or she paints. Edna Hibel sold her first painting during her years as a student at the Boston Museum School of Fine Arts. While she was there, her fellow students occasionally traded their own work for a sample of hers, although she regularly gave away her paintings and drawings to anyone who admired them.

It was a fellow student, a Mrs. Rosalind W. Levine, who was the first to buy a painting from Edna. The young artist had gone to the beach to work with watercolors on her own. She was attracted by some little girls playing in the sand, and quickly painted the scene.

Mrs. Levine recalls the day she bought that Hibel watercolor.

"It was during our rest period in art school that I saw Edna's painting of the beach scene. There was something fresh about it, a glimpse behind the figures to what it means to be a child playing in the sand. I loved it immediately and asked to buy it."

"You can have it!" Edna laughed. "You don't have to buy it."

"No, I don't want you to give me the picture. I want to buy it. How much do you want for it?"

"How about five dollars?" Edna asked.

"That's not enough," Rosalind objected. "This painting is worth more than that."

The first painting sold by Edna

Finally the two agreed on a price of ten dollars. For Mrs. Levine, the Hibel watercolor was, and is, a treasure. For Edna, it was another step toward a career in art.

Edna gained a lifelong friend and a sense of artistic worth when she sold that first painting. Her next sale was equally important, but in an entirely different way.

She was still studying in Boston at the time, working under the German master, Karl Zerbe, who took over when Yacovlev left. Zerbe, like Yacovlev, was an excellent teacher and an intellectual one. He had a very large art library in his office and would often invite Edna there to talk about art and use his books for reference. His favorite painter was Picasso, world-famous for his creative independence.

One of the exercises in creative independence that Karl Zerbe gave his students was to paint or sculpt independently, outside of class. These projects were to be completed in about a month and then brought to school for a critique during a class session.

Edna worked hard for an entire month to finish her out-of-class painting which she entitled simply "Oxen." It was a farm scene of a man holding a plow being pulled across a field by a team of oxen. The painting was a gouache, a type of watercolor which was a popular medium with artists before acrylics became available.

When Edna brought the finished canvas to school for review by the teacher, Zerbe was more than a little impressed. He studied it carefully, then declared that in his judgment it was the best student work of art ever done at the Boston Museum School of Fine Arts.

Edna's excitement was interrupted by a call from the school manager, Mrs. Amy Gibson, for her to go to the office.

As she stepped through the door, Mrs. Gibson said, "My dear, I would like to buy your out-of-class painting of the farmer plowing the field."

Painting in her studio, 1934

Edna couldn't believe it. Just minutes before she had heard Karl Zerbe say such wonderful things about that painting and now she was being asked to sell it.

"I burst into tears," Edna recalls, "which surprised me as much as it surprised Mrs. Gibson. I was so proud of what Zerbe had said about that painting, and now here was someone who wanted to buy it immediately. Why couldn't I just keep this one painting for myself, at least for a while? How could I let someone else own my very best achievement as an artist?

"I ran back to see Professor Zerbe and told him why Mrs. Gibson had called me to her office. The first thing he did was to get me to stop crying. Then he talked to me about the decison I had to make. He said I could look at it this way: If I thought I would never do a better painting than the one he had just critiqued, then he would advise me to keep it. But, if I thought I could and would do better work, then there was no need for me to hang on to it."

Karl Zerbe had made his point. Edna saw the logic of his words. "Of course I'm going to do better paintings!" she exclaimed.

"So I sold the painting," Edna continues, "and I learned something I still use in making decisions today. When someone wants to buy something I consider very special to me, I ask myself if I really think I will never do anything better. The answer is simple. I hope I can always do better! Letting go of what I consider my best work is much easier when I remember Karl Zerbe's remarks."

The Artist Matures

T hose five years at the Boston Museum School of Fine Arts were a time of great maturing for Edna, both as an individual and as an artist. She was still living at home, and even though her work at school kept her busy, she loved being with her family and doing things with them. She and her father played tennis almost every weekend and continued to be fierce competitors as well as close companions.

As she grew up, her family and friends remained very important to Edna and set a pattern for her life.

"I had many friends and kept active contact with them," she recalls. "I had tennis friends, painting friends, and just friendly friends. I was part of their inner circles and they were part of mine. We are still close after all these years."

"I always loved swimming," Edna continues, "and two or three of us would get together in the summer to swim at Hull, Massachusetts, where there were good beaches. I was captain of the girls' basketball team a group of us organized. I loved playing piano, too, especially duets: challenging things like Mozart or Beethoven. And I was an avid reader, not only about art and the great masters, but all sorts of biographies of interesting people. My friends and I went to museums, which I still enjoy every chance I get, no matter what city or country I am in. We went to the ballet and to the opera, so it was a well-rounded and busy period in my life.

"Another thing I did was paint portraits of my family and friends. I had an attic studio in our home and felt very arty and romantic working up there. I was going with Tod then and did stacks of sketches of him. Some of these are part of the Hibel Museum exhibits, as are those I did of close friends. I started doing portraits when I was thirteen and kept at it all through high school and art school."

Part of Edna's growth as an artist came from the assignments she was given by her art teachers requiring that she work in different mediums. One of these was a class in fresco. Fresco is a process of painting on wet plaster. The colors become part of the surface of the plaster when it dries. In the Renaissance period, fresco was used to decorate entire walls and ceilings, such as in the Vatican in Rome, Italy. Edna was among the first to use fresco for smaller paintings, called easel paintings, and grew to love the medium. She remembers her first attempt at a fresco.

"I had just started art school and was working with wet plaster on a large, high area. I was standing on a big block to reach it. I got so excited I stepped back to get a look at what I had done. That's one time when my enthusiasm hit bottom!"

The summer Edna was nineteen she enrolled in a class in watercolors with Eliot O'Hara at Goose Rocks Beach, Maine. Mr. O'Hara had seen Edna's paintings at the art school in Boston and on the strength of what he saw granted her a scholarship. As a result, she spent her vacation in Maine that year working solely in watercolors.

Edna says of that experience, "I enjoyed Mr. O'Hara's course especially because watercolor is what I called an 'accident' kind of painting. As you worked, you had to sort of take advantage of accidental effects that happened because of the watercolors themselves. But Mr. O'Hara was very mechanical minded and technical. Under his instruction, I learned that I could control what I did even in this medium and get the exact effects I was after."

Man of Patzcuaro, watercolor,
21¼" x 14½", 1939

Edna was only twenty-two in 1939 when she graduated from the Boston Museum School of Fine Arts, one of the youngest students ever to complete the school's five-year course. She was awarded the Ruth Sturtevant Fellowship which gave her a year's study abroad. The war in Europe made it impossible for her to go there to study, so Edna chose to go to Mexico.

Edna left for Mexico City in September accompanied by her mother. It was fortunate that Lena Hibel went along, because Edna became seriously ill with dysentery a few weeks after arriving in Mexico, and was able to spend only three months there.

Despite her illness, Edna did more paintings in those three months than any previous Fellowship student had done in a whole year. She immediately felt at home among the Mexican people and admired their gentle dignity and openness. The feeling of love was mutual. Although Edna didn't speak Spanish, she spoke the language of love, which was understood everywhere she went.

During much of her time in Mexico, Edna was too ill to leave the house to look for subjects to paint. Lena solved the problem by going out into the streets and bringing back people to pose for her daughter.

Orange Lady, watercolor, 24½" x 19¼", 1939, purchased by the Museum of Fine Arts, Boston, Frederick Brown Fund

27

"One day in Patzcuaro, Mom brought home a beggar to model for me. We found out later that he was the richest man in the village, and for good reason," Edna recounts. "He had the best spot in town for begging and he was very streetwise. The whole time he posed for me, he kept needing more and more money. But he had a fantastic face. I did three paintings of that face. All three are in the Hibel Museum.

"Another time, my Mom brought in a young woman she found on a street corner selling oranges. I was in the middle of doing the portrait of her when her husband came in and complained that his wife was losing money by sitting for me instead of selling oranges. So I paid for the oranges. Then I paid for the care of her baby at home. Every day there was a new reason for more money. To me, it was more than worth it. That painting was later purchased by the Boston Museum of Fine Arts for its permanent collection.

"I loved the people of Mexico in spite of the games some of them played in order to get money. Most of their needs were real, and they were as generous as they were needy. They have beautiful souls as well as beautiful faces."

Falling in Love

Meanwhile, a new interest had come into Edna's life: Tod Plotkin. Edna had known Tod since grammar school days when they were classmates at the Edward Devotion School in Brookline. When they graduated, she was thirteen, a tall, lanky girl almost full grown and several inches taller than Tod.

During their high school years, Tod caught up with Edna in height and grew to be "six feet tall and beautiful," as Edna puts it. He was a good athlete, especially in track events. Edna attended all the track meets to watch him and cheer his prowess and achievements in the long jump. The record he set in high school in that event helped get him into Harvard, where he planned to train for the Olympics. Then, in the final meet as a senior at Brookline High, Tod pulled a muscle and never fully recovered. He did go on to attend Harvard, but the muscle injury kept him out of college competition and ended his chance to take part in the Olympics.

The summer following their senior year of high school, Edna and Tod became more than just classmates and friends. They discovered each other. It happened almost by accident. Edna recalls the exact moment. Her story reveals much about the innocence and depth of their relationship.

"Tod and I spent a lot of time together that summer, mostly just walking the beach and talking. We never so much as held hands. One day, we were sitting on the beach talking away when we dug our fingers into the sand. Our fingers just sort of happened to touch. Suddenly the sparks flew! I had never felt anything like that before. Apparently Tod hadn't either. Neither of us moved. We were both literally shocked. I didn't realize that Tod felt as I did until much later when he admitted he had had the same feelings. Just like that, we were in love.

"We never talked about going together or being engaged or married. We both knew we were right for each other and that was the way it would always be. It does happen in real life just like it does in fairy tales. I know, because it happened to me."

Tod and Edna went together for six years before they were married. Tod was living in Cambridge and attending Harvard, while Edna was in Boston studying art. They were both too busy to see much of each other, leaving little more than summers together. In between, they were lonely.

After Tod Plotkin graduated from Harvard, he went to work for his father in New York to learn the buying end of the clothing business. Edna was in her last year at school.

Tod, making his record jump   *The young athlete, 1938*

Tod and Edna, leaning against Edna's 1935 Ford Roadster, "Terry"

They wrote to each other every day, even on Sunday when Tod's letters had to be special delivered to Edna's home. The whole family watched for those daily letters and were aware of what they meant to Edna.

She and Tod spent the summer of 1939 together. Then in September she went to Mexico on the Fellowship. Every hour was filled with painting and travelling, yet she missed Tod terribly. When she became ill with dysentery and had to leave Mexico, she had mixed feelings. She was sad to have had only three months for her Fellowship project in a country she had come to love so much, but she was glad she would again get to see Tod, whom she loved more than ever.

Edna and Lena Hibel returned to Brookline in December, allowing Tod and Edna to see each other frequently over the holidays. Edna knew that she wanted to become Tod's wife more than anything else. Tod felt the same way about her. They decided to get married as soon as possible. Their wedding took place one month later in January, 1940. They were both twenty-two years old and so much in love that apart from being together, nothing else mattered.

Wedding day, January 7, 1940

As Edna tells it, their honeymoon was "something else."

"Tod's mother and father were flying to Florida for a vacation and wanted their car there, so we drove it down for them. That was the start of our honeymoon trip. When we got to Florida, my folks were there too, so our stay was more like a family reunion than a romantic tryst. Neither of us cared. We were so happy to be together that we didn't even notice the rest of the family. As far as we were concerned, there was just Tod and me."

When they went back to Brookline, the young couple rented an apartment where Edna continued to paint, using the living room as a studio. They had only been married a short time when she became ill again with a relapse of the Mexican dysentery and had to stay in bed for months.

It was during that illness that Tod Plotkin developed an interest in Edna Hibel, the artist. Since she couldn't get out of bed, he brought her books on art and read them aloud to her. Tod tells this part of the story.

"At first I didn't pay much attention to what I was reading. I had chosen the books for Edna's sake, not for myself. Then, little by little, I came to understand the work of the great masters and the history of art. I saw the part that artistic expression played in the civilization of all races of people. I began to understand why Edna was excited by art, both seeing it and creating it. I had fallen in love with the girl I grew up with, a companion and friend who was as beautiful inside as out. During that illness, I learned to appreciate my wife as an artist, a very special and talented one. I became one of the most devoted Hibel followers, and I still am. Today, Edna and I frequently discuss the subject of art and I write about her career and artistic achievements."

Tod Plotkin also writes poetry, sensitive "paintings with the gift of speech" (as Simonides once said) that complement his wife's talent as an artist.

Tod took this picture by stretching out his arm, holding the camera.

The First Show

While Edna and Tod were honeymooning in Florida, three events took place that gave Edna's career a boost. First, her series of Mexican paintings was put on display at the Plotkin Bros. Department Store in Boston. Tod's cousin was in charge of window displays for the store and he thought the striking colors Edna used in that series would go well with the colors of the new fashions they were showing.

Robert Vose III, well-known art critic and director of the most prestigious art gallery in the Northeast, happened to walk by the Plotkin store, spied Edna's paintings in the window and immediately contacted Edna to arrange for a Hibel show at the Vose Gallery in Boston.

The third event made art history. The Boston Museum School of Fine Arts decided to hold a Hibel show in its exhibit hall. This was a "first" of some consequence for Edna.

Dr. George Edgell, the Director of the Boston Museum of Fine Arts, was invited to the show and was urged to attend. He was not very excited about going. He had been to so many students' shows that he did not expect to see anything out of the ordinary. Several weeks passed before he finally made it to the exhibit hall. Edgell was surprised and moved by Hibel's talent. He recognized that here at last was a student who more than fulfilled his greatest expectations for the school. He was so excited that he immediately chose two of the paintings on display and took them to the next meeting of the Museum's Board of Directors.

The meeting was held at the time of the year when the Board purchased new works of art for their collection. The members of the Board were as impressed as Dr. Edgell with the Hibel paintings he had brought along. They voted to buy one, an historic purchase that made Edna Hibel the youngest living artist to have a painting in the permanent collection of a major American art museum. She was twenty-three years old.

Edna's account of the event gives us insight into her personal character and her naive attitude toward her career.

"When Dr. Edgell told me about the Board's decision, we had quite a conversation over the price the museum should pay for that painting. I said I thought sixty dollars was top price. That sounded like a lot of money to me at the time, and in those days it was. Dr. Edgell disagreed with me. Sixty dollars might be all right for an art student, but I was no longer a student. I was an artist and I had better start thinking of myself as one. He told me in no uncertain terms that I was to ask at least one hundred and fifty dollars for any painting I sold from then on. I was so surprised I almost laughed in his face, but I did what he said."

Shortly after this conversation, Dr. Edgell purchased a Hibel painting from the Robert C. Vose Gallery for his own pleasure. His wife also bought a Hibel for her personal collection. These three paintings are now worth many, many times what was paid for them.

The show at the Robert C. Vose Gallery that spring was such a success that Robert Vose asked for a second show the following year. The date was set for the entire month of May, 1941. Edna was to have a whole series of new paintings ready for him by then. She planned to start on them immediately.

Shortly after the close of the first show, a recurrence of the Mexican dysentery sent Edna back to bed. This time she was too sick even to think of painting. Then another event interrupted her career: this one a blessed event. Edna was pregnant.

Between the dysentery and the pregnancy, Edna spent almost all of her time in bed unable to hold a brush. On April 7, 1941, she gave birth to her first-born son, Jonny. The second show for Robert Vose was a few weeks away and she had only ten paintings ready to exhibit. The situation seemed out of hand. Edna called her mother for help.

"How can I help?" Lena Hibel asked in response to Edna's plea. "I'm not an artist!"

"No, but you are a grandmother! How would you like to come and take care of Jonny while I paint?"

So Edna and Lena worked as a team to make the May 1 deadline. Early every morning, Lena picked up the baby and kept him all day while Edna worked in her studio. Late each afternoon Lena would return and exchange Jonny for the painting Edna had finished. Then Lena drove to Boston to have the new canvas framed, rushed back home to get dinner for Abraham and herself, and was there to take the baby for Edna the next morning.

For two weeks Edna and her mother kept to this exhausting schedule. It took all their strength, determination and talent, but they met the deadline right to the minute. By May 1, Edna had twenty-five paintings framed and ready to show. The exhibit was even more successful than the first, with an opening that was an unforgettable celebration.

Coincidently there was an exhibit of paintings by Alexander Yacovlev, along with Edna's paintings. Edna had arrived! There were the works of teacher and student hanging side by side.

Career Versus Family

Edna's career as an artist made progress in spite of her growing responsibility as a wife and mother. She had the good fortune, she says, to always seem to meet the right person at the right time.

After the first Boston show, Edna was introduced to Mrs. McKinley Helm whose husband was an established and respected art critic and writer. Mrs. Helm arranged for her husband to meet Edna and see the work she was doing.

"I went to that meeting without bringing a single canvas with me," Edna admits, shaking her head as she relates the story. "Of course, Dr. Helm asked to see some of my work. I didn't have anything to show him, so all I could do was tell him about my three months in Mexico and try to describe a few of the things I had done there. He listened to what I had to say about my paintings and then let me have it. 'Frankly, they sound like something I would definitely hate!' he said."

Edna was stunned by his words, but she decided that if the art critic could be blunt with her, she could be blunt with him.

"You certainly have a right to hate my paintings, or any other artist's painting, if you want to," she told McKinley Helm, "but it seems to me that you should at least look at them first!"

"I don't have to see what you've done to know that I don't like American artists who go to another country to get inspiration for their paintings," Dr. Helm replied.

The conversation ended there. Edna figured that her paintings had had it as far as one art critic was concerned. Events proved she was wrong.

One day during that hectic two weeks when Edna was trying to get her paintings finished for the second Vose Gallery show, Lena Hibel rushed into the frame shop in Boston with two canvases to be made ready to hang in the exhibit. Dr. Helm happened to walk into the shop at the same time. He had no idea that Lena was Edna Hibel's mother. He only knew that he liked the paintings she was having framed. In fact, he liked them very much. One was a small oil on board of Jonny at the age of one month. The other was a scene Edna had sketched in Mexico.

"Who is the artist who did these fascinating paintings?" he asked, introducing himself.

"They are the work of my daughter, Edna Hibel," Lena said. "I think you met her a few weeks ago," she couldn't resist adding.

Dr. Helm wasted no time calling Edna to apologize for his rude criticism of her work before he had even seen it. "If they have not already been sold, I would like to buy both of the paintings your mother had at the frame shop."

Edna with Jonny, Andy and Dicky, 1951

38

The Mexican scene had been sold, but Dr. Helm was able to buy the oil of Jonny. He is still the proud owner of it as part of his Hibel collection in his museum in Santa Barbara, California.

Not long after this happened, McKinley Helm wrote a comment about the paintings Edna had done in Mexico and said that she had truly put her finger on the soul of the people. In his judgment, she had found "her signature," her own style of art, at a very early age.

In spite of Dr. Helm's favorable review, for the next eighteen years Edna Hibel's career took second place in her life. She gave birth to two more sons, Andy in 1947 and Richard, called Dicky, in 1950. Second place, however, did not mean that those hands of hers had lost their talented touch. It simply meant that along with holding paintbrushes and palette, they held diapers, laundry baskets, and shopping bags full of groceries.

For a time the Hibel creative instinct was dormant, but it was far from dead. Edna painted every moment she could spare, even if it was only for twenty minutes at a time.

Once in a while, however, art did come first. Two years after Jonny was born, the Norton Gallery in West Palm Beach, Florida bought a Hibel painting for its permanent collection. This meant that there were now three Hibels in permanent collections of fine art galleries.

Another milestone event for Edna was her first one-artist show in New York City at the John Levy Gallery. Even so, Edna was still too busy with the children to take time for other shows. Although she was included in the 1940-41 edition of *Who's Who in American Art*, she didn't even hear about that surprising bit of public recognition until several years later.

*Lena and Edna go for a ride in
Palm Beach*

It was 1954 before Edna's career as an artist came into the spotlight again. It began with a one-artist show at the DeCordova Museum in Lincoln, Massachusetts. This was a large retrospective exhibit, the first of its kind of Hibel paintings. It looked back to her earliest work as well as to what she was doing then.

Later that same year, Edna was credited with organizing the first Boston Arts Festival. This festival was one of the most important art events in the United States and attracted artists and collectors from all parts of the country. In those days, the artists in and around Boston had no place where they could hold an open air exhibit. A group of them got together and decided that the best place to hold such an event would be the Boston Public Garden in the Back Bay area. However, when they went to the city officials to ask for the site, they were turned down.

Edna heard about what happened and organized the artists' efforts. She worked tirelessly to bring them together with the Back Bay officials and the city mayor. Eventually, the first Boston Arts Festival took place in the Public Garden and Edna was recognized as the prime founder. This show was held for many years and was recognized as one of the largest and most popular in the art world.

Two years later, Edna's career was given another boost. Her paintings were chosen to be included in the American Federation of Art's travelling exhibit, a collection taken to many cities throughout the United States. Edna doesn't recall exactly what cities were on that tour. She was still too busy being a wife and mother to concentrate on a full-time career as an artist.

The DeCordova Museum exhibit featured a retrospective of her earlier work.

Important Changes

B etween 1954 and 1960, the stage was set for some of the most important changes in Edna's personal life and career. The Plotkin Bros. Department Store, which had been experiencing difficulties, finally closed its doors. The family was left with many debts. Tod felt he should help pay them. Edna started giving art lessons at home to bring in extra money. She also sold the few paintings she had time to complete.

One day, her youngest son, Dicky, almost spoiled a much needed sale. At the age of five he already had shown great sensibility to art. He had started his own museum in the attic where he displayed shells, rocks, pictures, photos, sculptures, relics from museums, fossils, and more. He wrangled small paintings from his mother as well by saying, "You wouldn't give that to me for my museum, would you?"

A patron, who was aware of the family's financial straights and wanted to be helpful, selected two small paintings for purchase. As Edna was delivering them to her at the door, Dicky came by and saw what was happening. He grabbed his mother around the legs and howled, "Those are the ones I wanted." Sorry to say, those paintings did not end up in his museum. However, they have since been donated to the Hibel Museum of Art.

Then in December of 1959, Abraham Hibel died. Edna felt a deep loss. Even more devastating, Lena fell apart over her husband's death. For the first time in Lena's sixty-two years, she could not see the bright side of anything.

Edna's family and her career were tied up in her mother's grief. It hung over everything and everyone like a black cloud.

As usual with Edna, something happened to break through the gloom and open up a new future for Edna and Lena.

One morning a few months after Abraham's death, a friend telephoned Edna to tell her about a store that had become vacant in Rockport, Massachusetts. Rockport was a popular artist's colony known all over the United States. The friend suggested Rockport would be the perfect place for a Hibel gallery. Edna relates what happened.

"I had never thought of owning a gallery. What on earth would I do with it if I had it? I didn't even think of myself as an artist. How could I manage a gallery and when would I find time to paint enough pictures to fill it?

"I didn't tell Tod about the call immediately. It just seemed like such an impossible suggestion it wasn't worth talking about. There were too many questions about owning a gallery for which I didn't have answers. I forgot about the call and went to bed.

"During the night I woke up as if I had been shaken. Suddenly I had the answer to all those questions about a gallery in Rockport. My mother! Lena needed something really exciting to do. She could run the gallery for us. It might be just the thing to get her out of her awful slump.

"I didn't wait until daylight to talk to Tod about it. I woke him up right then. It was three o'clock in the morning, but Tod shared my excitement. My mother was as special to him as she was to me. He was willing to try anything that might help her start living again."

At six o'clock the next morning, Edna and Tod put in a call to Lena. "How would you like to manage an art gallery for us?" they asked.

Lena was gloomy. "What do I know about running a gallery?"

"But we need you, Mom!" Edna and Tod insisted.

They told her about the friend's call and the chance they had to rent a wonderful gallery in Rockport. They couldn't afford to pass up the opportunity, they said. All they needed was Lena's willingness to be a charming hostess and take charge of the place for them.

Lena, though full of doubts, finally agreed.

Edna and Tod hung up the telephone and celebrated. At least Lena was willing to try. That alone was good news. A few hours later they were on their way to Rockport to see the vacant store. The village itself looked like a picture postcard. They couldn't wait to see where their art gallery would be located.

When they found the place, they were shocked and disappointed. The building was a huge, abandoned supermarket. "In fact," says Edna, "it was a huge, abandoned super mess!" Nevertheless, Edna and Tod took the Hibel future in their hands and signed the lease.

For the next two weeks they worked night and day to clean up the mess. With the help of a friend they scrubbed, painted and polished. Tod borrowed movable panels which he used to divide the yawning space of the interior into smaller areas to get rid of the supermarket look. The floor was partly covered with two Oriental rugs they brought from home. Finally the place was ready to hang pictures.

Just as they expected, Edna did not have nearly enough paintings to cover the almost endless length of bare walls. She didn't let this trouble her for long. She went to people who had bought Hibel paintings and borrowed them to fill up wall space. At last, she and Tod were ready to bring Lena to see her gallery.

In June of 1960, the Edna Hibel Gallery on Main Street in Rockport opened for business with Lena at the helm. Neither Edna nor Tod was sure it would be a financial suc-

Tod, Lena and Edna select frames made by Tod.

cess. As far as they were concerned it didn't matter at the start if people came to buy the paintings. It only mattered that Lena was kept busy so she would become outgoing and happy again.

"Now don't worry about selling paintings," Tod told Lena again and again. "That can come later, after the gallery is established. All we want you to do is welcome visitors and make them feel at home."

There was only one rule that Tod insisted Lena must follow: "Just in case someone wants to buy a painting, you are not to sell anything for less than the price we have marked on it."

When Lena saw the prices on the artwork, she questioned them. The prices were modest even for the times, but to Lena they seemed like far too much to ask. She had been around Edna's paintings all her life, yet this was the first time she had ever noticed what they sold for. She was sure no one would pay from $50 to $200 for something you could only hang on a wall.

Even though she was worried about the prices, Lena had an unusual dream the night before the gallery opened.

"I dreamt that someone came into the gallery and bought every last painting we had for sale. It seemed so real, even though I knew it was just a wild and unrealistic dream. When I told Edna and Tod the next morning, we all laughed about it."

A few hours after the gallery opened with Lena in charge, she called Tod to tell him that a lovely couple wanted to buy one of Edna's paintings but could only afford half of what was being asked. "Can I sell it for half-price?" she asked.

Tod had expected that this would happen. He had to tell Lena "No," even though it was one of the hardest things he ever had to say to her.

"We can't do that," he explained patiently. "Remember what I said about the one rule you were to follow? Nothing is to be sold for less than it is marked."

Within the hour, the telephone rang again. Tod was afraid it would be Lena. It was. This time she was so excited she could hardly talk.

"Guess what?" she burst out in a high voice. "I just sold that painting for the full price! You were right! I can't believe it, but you were right!"

That was Lena's first sale of the day. It was not her last. Before the season at Rockport was over, she had sold every-thing in the gallery. She even sold the two Oriental rugs on the floor. Lena Hibel had found "her signature."

The most important sale Lena made took place on her second day at the Main Street gallery. Ethelbelle and Clayton B.

Craig came in to look around and see what was on exhibit. They immediately fell in love with Lena and with her daughter's paintings. Before they left the gallery that afternoon, the Craigs bought five Hibels.

"We didn't bring our checkbook with us," they apologized, "so will you hold these five paintings until we can drive home and come back with a check for you?"

"You don't have to leave the paintings here," Lena replied. "Just take them with you and bring the check back later."

"You can't do business that way!" Mr. and Mrs Craig objected. "How can you trust us just like that?"

Lena insisted it was all right. "I don't have to worry about people with faces as beautiful as yours."

So the Craigs took their paintings and went to get a check to pay for them while Lena got on the telephone and called Edna and Tod.

"Sit down," she warned. "I have something to tell you."

Edna and Tod didn't know quite what to expect.

"I just sold five Hibels! To one customer!"

Edna and Tod were speechless, but not Lena. She was bubbling with news. She told them all about the Craigs and

Clayton and Ethelbelle Craig

how they and everyone who came into the gallery were responding with high praise for Edna's paintings.

"Isn't it wonderful!" she finished excitedly.

To Edna and Tod, it was more then wonderful. It was almost a miracle to hear Lena sounding like herself again, her happy, exuberant self.

Ethelbelle and Clayton B. Craig would in time become the owners of one hundred and eighty Hibel paintings. They were so proud of their collection that they found wall space to hang every one of them. That collection and the Craigs' generosity were later behind the most historic step in Edna Hibel's career.

Lena continued to sell things as fast as Edna could paint them and Tod could get them to Rockport. What the grandmother-turned-saleswoman lacked in business experience, she made up for in charm and enthusiasm. When the gallery closed that fall, everyone agreed it had been a most successful and wise venture, anyway you looked at it.

When winter set in, Lena had time on her hands again, but not for long. Edna and Tod sent her off on another adventure, this time to Boston to find a site for a new gallery on Newbury Street, the city's art center. Lena put her heart into the search and came up with exactly the right place. Very shortly thereafter, she was busy selling again at the new Edna Hibel Gallery in Boston.

With two galleries and a super saleswoman to keep supplied with paintings, Edna had a new worry. Where would she find time to create the artwork needed to keep up with those demands year round? Tod was working long hours at a furniture factory job, and while Jonny was away at college, Andy and Richard were still at home. Edna needed to free herself from household duties that kept her away from her studio. It was decision time again.

Mexican Beggar, oil on canvas,
50" x 36"

Two Brothers, oil and gesso on plasterboard,
11" x 10"

Greek Dancers, oil fresco, 16" x 28½"

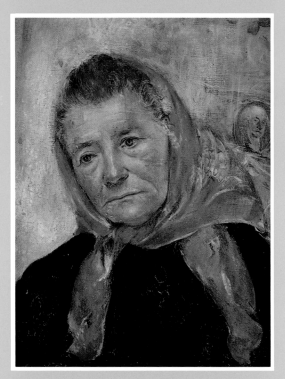

*My Grandmother, egg underpainting and
oil glazes on aluminum panel, 14" x 10"*

Tulips, oil on canvas, 40″ x 30″

Africa, conte crayon and nupastel on paper, 31½″ x 24¾″

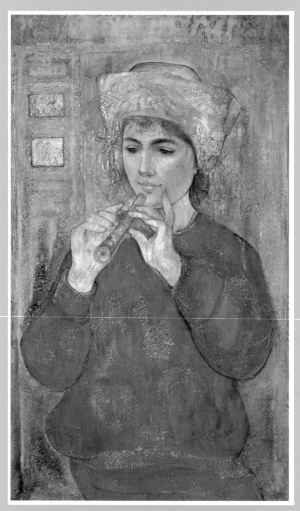

Recorder, oil fresco, 42" x 25¾"

Veronique and Child, oil and gesso on silk, 24" x 20½"

Three proofs of progressions in lithograph

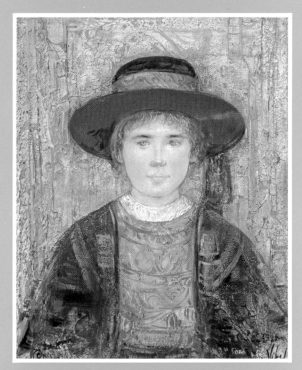

Breton Boy, oil and gesso on silk, 22" x 16"

Elsa, oil and gesso on silk, 9³/₈" x 9³/₈"

Quisisana, oil on silk,
22¾″ x 13¾″

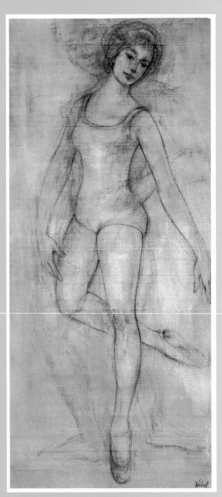

Ballerina, charcoal on silk, 48″ x 26″

Sami, pencil drawing on cameo paper

Mother and Children, oil and charcoal on silk, 36" x 30"

A selection from the new ceramic art created by Edna in Umbria, Italy

Celestial Bridge, bone china sculptures

Donna and Children, crystal relief

Garden Belle, porcelain doll in the Rosalie Collection

His Majesty's Treasure Chest, English bone china sculpture

A Portrait of Edna, taken at her studio on Singer Island, by Kaufman

Art Comes First at Last

The big decision was made by Edna and Tod on November 23, 1963. That was the day after the assassination of President John F. Kennedy. Edna and Tod were in shock over the tragedy. It made them realize how uncertain the future could be. They talked about their own lives and what they were doing with them. By then, Tod had come to truly appreciate Edna's talent as an artist. He felt it was time to organize their plans and efforts around that important fact and give her career the focus it deserved and needed.

During their talk that November afternoon, Tod put his feelings into words. "My job is just that, a job. It is something that keeps me away from home, away from you and the boys. Now, if I stayed home and took over the responsibility of the house and the business end of the galleries, you would be free to paint without constant interruptions. That's what you should be doing. Who knows where your career will take you if we both give it a chance to be first in our lives?"

Edna listened with mixed emotions. To put her opportunity as an artist above her duties as a wife and mother was not easy. It went against the traditions she had grown up with about a woman's place in life. The idea of a marriage partnership focusing on her career seemed almost selfish. But something inside of her jumped at the thought of having time to really paint again. Their patron friends, the Craigs, convinced them the time was right. It was worth a try.

With that decision made, Edna and Tod took over their new roles with a sense of adventure. They were together again, working hard toward a goal they shared with joy, in a partnership they knew was right for them. There was a lot to do, but they had enough time and talent between them to do it, and do it well. And they had love. As always, love was behind everything in their lives.

At last Edna's career was truly free to go forward. She decided that before the world could come to know her, she had to come to know the world and its people. She had to become familiar with the master artists of the past whose work paved the way for her own career in art. The year was 1963 and there was peace abroad, so she and Tod packed up the family and went to Europe.

Their first stop was Portugal where a number of Edna's own paintings were "born" of the inspiration which came to her from the spirit and grace of the people. During her short visit, Edna captured on canvas the soul of Portugal and the Portuguese ethos.

After Portugal came Italy. Edna immersed herself in the ancient land with its sunny climate and people. For the first time, she was studying great art where it was created by the revered masters of the Old World.

That trip to Europe was the first of many abroad. Everywhere she went, Edna fell in love all over again. Her artistic self reached out in France, England, Holland, Switzerland, Greece and Spain as it had in Portugal and Italy to fill her senses with images and feelings that were to keep her hands busy for years.

"I found a special quality in each town and village we visited," Edna comments. "I couldn't wait to paint what I saw."

Meanwhile, back in the United States, Edna's career was on the move. Before leaving for Europe, Edna went to Sarasota, Florida to find a new gallery so Lena wouldn't run out of things to do while the family was abroad. The Edna Hibel Gallery

Fisherwoman of Nazaré, oil on canvas, 48" x 40", Portugal, 1965

in Sarasota opened in January, 1964. That was late for the tourist season, but not too late for Lena to do very well.

When she closed the Sarasota gallery for the summer, Lena left some of Edna's paintings at the Frank Oehlaschlaeger Gallery across the street. Mr. Oehlaschlaeger had been interested in the Hibel exhibit ever since it came to Sarasota and was hoping he could handle Edna's work all year round. When Lena headed back to re-open the gallery in Rockport, she felt she left the door open for new things to happen in Florida.

Lena was right. Things did happen. The very next year, Frank Oehlaschlaeger held the first of a series of one-artist Hibel exhibits in Sarasota. That was followed by another one-artist exhibit at the Harmon Gallery in Naples, Florida. Then Mr. Oehlaschlaeger set a date for an exclusive Hibel show at his gallery in Chicago. That event and a one-artist show at the Kenmore Gallery in Philadelphia meant that recognition of Edna's work was spreading far and wide.

Things were happening so fast that it was hard to get Edna's paintings framed in time for shows. Tod decided to try his hand at the task of framing. He soon became so good at it that Hibels are now among the most beautifully-framed canvases to be found anywhere. Tod, too, was finding his signature.

Edna continued to paint under her maiden name of Hibel. Sometimes this caused minor mix-ups that the family joked about. Occasionally the kids at school teased Andy and Richard about being Hibels instead of Plotkins. Once in a while Tod himself was mistakenly called "Mr. Hibel." That still happens.

"Why should I object?" Tod asks philosophically. "If a woman can give up her maiden name to share that of her husband for family reasons, then a man should be able to share his wife's maiden name if it is practical for professional or any other reason."

Tod and their sons know Edna is Mrs. Plotkin. So do their friends and close associates. Most important, so does Edna. Success has not changed that fact one tiny bit.

Adventure in Lithography

One of Edna Hibel's biggest challenges and greatest adventures as an artist came when she "discovered" lithography, the art of making original graphics by drawing on stone. The word comes from the Greek "lithos," meaning stone, and "graph," meaning written. It is an old art form dating back to 1795, but it was brand new to Edna in 1966 when a friend talked her into going to the workshop of George Lockwood, a lithographer in Boston.

"I went intending to do just one lithograph to please my friend," Edna admits, "but before I left that day I had begun drawings on six different stones."

When she ran her hands over the smooth surfaces of the limestone as she got ready to do her first drawing, the feel of that stone under her sensitive fingers sparked Edna's imagination.

"Who knows how many years, how many eons of time and how much creative force went into the making of this stone?" she asked herself.

The experience almost moved her to tears.

"I felt an awe for the drama that must have taken place during the span of centuries in which the stone was formed," Edna recalls. "I saw it as a natural work of art. How could I dare to improve on what it had taken millions of years to achieve?"

That thought made Edna feel humble and reverent, but it was also exciting.

"I was inspired as well as thrilled by the newness of this medium. The creative urge was so strong I could hardly wait to start drawing. From the moment I held a grease crayon in my hand and made that first stroke, I couldn't pull myself away. I turned to my first love, the mother and child theme, and I was delighted with the results I was able to get on stone.

"I began by sketching a woman's face, not any particular woman unless maybe it was a figurative image of Mother Earth herself. The expression I wanted was one of deep and constant caring. After all, Mother Earth had cared for so many life forms for so long. Then I quickly added a child to the picture to make the woman a mother."

Edna was fascinated as she watched her first stone being "pulled." To pull a stone means that the drawing surface of the stone is covered with ink, then paper is pressed down over the inked surface leaving a print of the drawing on the paper.

Edna held her breath when she saw what was being done to her first drawing on stone.

"I had sketched the figures of the mother and child with such care, and there they were using a heavy roller to spread black ink all over it. Fortunately, I didn't have long to wait. The stone was covered with paper, then they were run through the press together. And there was my first lithograph!"

Final corrections at studio in Zurich

Edna's adventure in lithography continued a few years later in Zurich, Switzerland, at a studio called Wolfensberger Graphi Anstalt, where she went to perfect her grasp of the medium. Some of the world's master lithographers work at Wolfensberger's. She still goes there every year and works with two masters of the craft.

The stones Edna uses in Zurich come from Solnoven, Bavaria, and are from the same limestone quarries used in 1795 by Alois Senefelder, the inventor of lithography. Senefelder's invention was almost immediately adopted by many artists because his method makes possible the best quality multiple prints of an original painting or drawing.

To create a lithograph, Edna first choses the stone on which she wants to work. No two slabs of limestone are alike, even those quarried from the same source and ground to the same smoothness. Each stone retains a special character which the artist can "read" as her hands touch and explore the surface. When her mind comes alive with an idea or image ready for impression, Edna begins to draw. Each image takes on a life of its own on that particular stone.

After a drawing is finished, an acid and gum arabic solution is applied to the surface of the limestone, so that when an oil-based ink is rolled onto the stone, it adheres only to those areas where the artist has drawn with a greasy medium. Apart from the artist's drawing itself, it is the most important step in creating a lithograph.

Every time a new color is added to a lithograph, a new drawing must be rendered on a fresh stone. That color is then added to the impression of the original drawing. In the book *Museum Suite*, published by Tod Plotkin, you can see the sixteen separate steps used in creating "Okasan to Kodoma," one of Edna Hibel's lithographs. As you turn the pages, you can see how the colors are added, one at a time. The beauty

Edna working on a stone

of the finished work evolves as each different shade of color is added.

A wide range of effects is possible to an artist willing to spend hours, and even days, experimenting with different combinations of colors.

"Sometimes I wish my brain were a computer," Edna wrote recently. "Then I could figure out all of the millions of wonderful combinations that are possible."

Edna's willingness to experiment, combined with her keen artistic sense, is a part of what makes her lithographs so notable. There is an infinite variety in the choices of stone, colors, and paper for each print, and Edna has become a master in selecting exciting combinations.

In the Foreword of the book entitled *Hibel Lithographs*, Edna writes, "Drawing has enthralled me since my early teens. I feel it is basic to all graphic art. The fascination of the drawing technique required in lithography, combined with the puzzle of putting several stones together to get unique color effects from the grease inks, captivated me. And, of course, the deeper I delve into these problems the more ideas keep emerging. The more you learn, the more you want to learn.

"I have much to look forward to."

An Important Move

Edna and Tod moved their home base from Boston to Florida in 1970, but they had begun pulling up their roots five years earlier. Edna's career was thriving in Florida, and with the boys practically grown, she and Tod were spending a lot more time there. Gradually it became natural to think of that state as "home." Even the weather there was friendly.

It was on their way back east from a one-artist show at the Harmon Gallery in Naples that Edna and Tod talked about opening a second gallery in Florida. They were thinking more of Lena than of anything else. She seemed to be heading for a slump again, and they couldn't let that happen.

"Why don't we open a new gallery for her in Palm Beach?" suggested Edna. "Mom loves the weather down here and she needs a new challenge to keep her going."

"Like someone else I know!" Tod teased.

They had driven about one hundred miles north of Palm Beach at that point, but Tod turned the car around and headed back. It was eleven o'clock that night before they found a motel and got to a telephone. They called Lena who was still at the exhibit in Naples.

"What have you two thought up for me now?" Lena asked when Edna and Tod told her to meet them in Palm Beach the next morning.

"You'll see," they promised.

It didn't take long to sell Lena on the idea of a gallery in Palm Beach. The three of them went looking for a location. They found an empty building on Worth Avenue that was just what they needed. The following morning they signed a lease. Edna left immediately for Massachusetts to start painting, while Tod and Lena stayed in Florida to make plans for a grand opening in two weeks.

"It was another of those crazy two weeks of ours," Edna laughs. "We could have picked a later date for the opening, but no, we had to do it in two weeks. I was in the studio from 5 a.m. until all hours of the night trying to make that deadline.

"Fortunately I can sit or stand in front of my easel and paint all day and not want to stop until I have to eat or sleep. There are many times when I have to force myself to lay down my brushes. The flow of ideas and the excitement I feel to paint them are always ahead of the hours I have to get it done."

The Palm Beach gallery was everything they hoped it would be, and more. Lena had plenty to keep her busy and therefore happy. She was the best advertisement the Hibel paintings could ever want. The crowds at the new gallery were bigger than ever. Lena's success at Palm Beach helped make the final decision for Edna and Tod to move from Massachusetts to Florida. They bought a home north of Palm Beach and made it their permanent address.

Shortly after the move, Edna and Tod left their new home and went to the Orient so Edna could study and paint in Japan.

"I had always loved, studied, and painted Oriental art and culture," she says of the trip. "The Boston Museum has a very large Oriental collection. While I was in school there I spent a lot of time in that section of the museum. Then, too, Boston has a big district called 'Chinatown' where there has always been a mixture of Oriental people. I used to go there every chance I had, so when I got to Japan I felt right at home."

The varied differences in people in the Far East made a lasting impression on Edna. Her love for people was her passport into the heart and spirit of the countries she visited.

Japanese Family, oil fresco on canvas, 48" x 30"

It is to her credit that she never met a "foreigner." Friendliness, kindness and compassion are not foreign to her. She sees those qualities wherever she goes. Love is always the first thing Edna experiences when her plane touches down in a new land.

If we keep coming back to the word "love" as we explore the life and art of Edna Hibel, it is because that single quality best describes the substance of her work and everything about her. Love, especially the bond between mother and child, is a subject Edna has never been able to put behind her and leave alone. She never tires of it. Her medium and techniques change, but not her motto about love: "You *can* take it with you!"

Edna painting Shizue, in 1958

Another New Medium

In 1972, Edna learned of yet another medium she had not tried, that of creating collector plates. When she was approached in 1971 by a respresentative of Royal Doulton, the world's famous fine china manufacturer, to do a painting for a series of collector plates, Edna had said, "I don't do dishes." Actually, she had not heard of collector plates. The practice of creating art on porcelain was long-established when Edna did her initial plate. In 1895, a Danish porcelain house issued the first holiday plate. When Royal Copenhagen came out with a Christmas plate seven years later, the popular business of plate collecting was launched.

No one was surprised when Edna "discovered" art on porcelain.

"I had never looked closely at a plate before," Edna admitted in an interview for *Plate World Magazine*, "so I wasn't interested in the medium because I didn't know what it was all about. But when I did notice the look of the porcelain, its translucency, it was exactly the look I was working to get in my paintings, those translucent layers of color. This is why porcelain has been fantastic for me, an absolutely natural medium."

Edna was asked if she had trouble learning to work within the limits of a plate. Was it hard to work within the confinement of a circle?

"No," she says, "my paintings lend themselves to a circle because I think in terms of interaction, interrelationship."

She goes on to explain, "My favorite subject is the mother-and-child motif and that is encircling. To me, this is the world, this encircling relationship. It is life.

"For example, the feeling mothers have for their babies, and the babies' reactions to their mothers, is the same all over the world. Mothers handle their babies differently, but with exactly the same feeling. I love that feeling and that's what I try to get. One of the ways of getting it is in a circle. To me, love is a circular thing."

Edna's first collector plate series was called "Mother and Child" and was issued by Royal Doulton of England starting in 1973 and ending in 1981. Today Edna is still working on a number of collector plate series with the same theme. One is the "International Mother Love" edition. Another is the "Mother's Day" tribute first issued in 1984. An unusual fact about this series is that the firing of each plate stops the day before Mother's Day the year it is issued and is never repeated. That means each edition is very limited.

Mother and Child plate

Working on a new plate, 1983

In 1985, Edna did her first "Hibel Christmas" plate. The scene was a typical mother-child painting with a powerful message of the spirit of peace, joy, and love which every religion holds sacred. Then came two other series, "The World I Love," and "Famous Women and Children," which also centered on the circular theme, as did one plate from the "David" series inspired by Edna's trip to Israel. In typical Hibel fashion, an outpouring of series has followed, exploring her favorite themes from the broad perspective of experiences such as "Tribute to All Children," "Eroica," "To Life," "Scandinavian Mother and Child," and more. . . always more.

Every Hibel plate, like every Hibel canvas, begins with an image she feels intuitively. When the vision is clear and complete, her hands begin to execute. Only on rare occasions does she do a sketch first. Most of the time, the image and her sense of it are so strong that the combination seems almost to reproduce itself to create the finshed piece.

Edna prefers to work in complete silence so she can concentrate fully on what she is doing. She works on several paintings at the same time. As soon as the initial burst of inspiration for a new idea comes to her, she leaves what she was doing to work on her new project as quickly as she can. She goes back and forth from painting to painting until she is satisfied.

The Hibel studio is part of the Plotkin home in Palm Beach County. To reach her studio you walk through the family room past rows of African violets in full bloom. There is no wall separating the studio from the living quarters, so Edna's studio is plainly visible through the open archway.

The studio is filled with frames and art supplies, cartons of them piled on the floor and on shelves. Leaning against the cartons are unfinished paintings, rough sketches, and drawings waiting for her to pick up and complete when she has the time and inspiration. A clay sculpture, one of her latest projects, sits on a pedestal nearby. An unfinished doll, the most recent in Edna's large collection, waits for the artist's final touches.

On one side of the room is a floor-to-ceiling window that looks out on the patio bordering the lake. The view itself is like a painting. Edna wears a smock and sits in front of the window. Her eyes are intent on the canvas before her. Within easy reach is a supply of oil paints, boxes of them spread out over the surface of the work bench. Also within reach are her old tennis trophies which she now uses as vases to hold the bouquets of paintbrushes she must have at hand.

When she is working, nothing disturbs Edna's concentration. She paints quickly, easily and carefully. The telephone at her elbow rings, and, almost without missing a stroke, she reaches out with her left hand and holds the phone to her ear. She continues to paint with her right hand as she carries on a conversation. Her eyes never leave the canvas. She is at the same time totally at peace and excited about her work.

It is obvious that this artist, this woman, loves what she is doing.

At work in the studio

In the spring of 1976, while Edna was working in her studio, something happened that almost ended her career. Suddenly she had trouble seeing with her right eye. The vision was clouded by strange, blinding flashes of light and dark spots.

"I was scared to death!" Edna admits as she tells what happened.

The doctor diagnosed a torn retina, a serious threat for anyone, but even more frightening for an artist. The doctor gave Edna drops to put in both eyes every afternoon, causing her vision to blur. This meant that she could only paint in the morning. The treatment went on for days. Finally, the doctor was able to repair the torn retina. Edna went back to work full-time in her studio, thinking the problem was behind her.

That summer, she and Tod were in Boston where Edna was busier than ever getting ready for her presentation to Queen Elizabeth. She was also doing her first "Oriental Gold" collector plate and the first "Nobility of Children" series. As if that were not enough, she was working in her spare time with Tod and the family on the color film, "Edna Hibel–The World I Love."

All at once, Edna experienced an explosion of flashing light and dark spots in her right eye. Tod took her directly to the hospital where she was examined by a specialist. After several days, he decided an operation was necessary to prevent any further damage to the retina.

Post-surgery recovery forced Edna to lie flat on her back for six weeks. She couldn't even use a pillow. She couldn't so much as move her head from side to side.

"It was such a long time, those six weeks," she recalls. "I couldn't paint, of course, and that was very bad. The doctor was amazed at how I followed his orders exactly. He said I was a very patient patient. I told him it wasn't patience, I was just too scared to move! In fact, I was terrified. What if I lost the sight of that right eye? Blindness is the worse thing that can happen to an artist."

Today, both the vision in her eyes and the vision in her heart and mind are leading Edna to work harder than ever. As in other crises during Edna's life, Tod was by her side and a constant source of support and encouragement to her.

Their relationship reached a new plateau when he started writing haiku, short lyric poems, usually seventeen syllables, originally a Japanese form. Like the touching of their fingers buried in sand when they fell in love, their creative talents touched when they collaborated on the book, *The Sundial Ticking*, published in 1978. Tod wrote the haiku. Edna did the paintings. The blend of art forms still brings pleasure to Edna and Tod, and to Hibel/Plotkin fans everywhere.

Poems by Theodore (Tod) Plotkin
from *The Sundial Ticking*

Spring morning
My wife sits down beside me
And says, "Hi."

Seated on the ground
Tending the flowers
A wisp of her hair stirs in the breeze.

The rain that falls silently
on the grass
Drums on my roof.

Come in butterfly,
the fence is not for you.

Summer sun
Setting slowly
Hanging on to today.

Several selections from The Sundial Ticking, *along with one of*
Edna's prints from the book, done in oil on cameo paper

The Hibel Museum of Art

Many artists who become a success have a friend or patron in the background, someone with vision and the means to get the world to sit up and take notice. Lena Hibel and Tod Plotkin were both an important part of Edna's success. But there were two other people to whom she owes much: Ethelbelle and Clayton B. Craig.

Mr. and Mrs. Craig did not meet Edna and Tod until three years after they had purchased those five paintings from Lena at Rockport in 1960. When they finally became acquainted, their initial feelings about Edna were confirmed.

They were invited to Brookline so they could meet the artist and her family and to see some of the new paintings which were ready to go on exhibit. They drove up to the house at about two o'clock that afternoon. Andy was having a piano lesson, and Dicky, a cello lesson, when they arrived. That was only part of what was happening. Later, Mr. Craig recalled that visit.

"It was a madhouse. People everywhere. It was dangerous to go up or down the stairs which were used to stack paintings and frames. Edna came out and told us that Mabel had dinner on the table and that we were staying. We didn't argue."

The family loved the Craigs immediately and the feeling was mutual. They came to visit often. Dicky liked them so much that he even wrote them a letter inviting them to dinner every night.

That first visit set a pattern for a warm friendship apart from the Craigs' patronage of Edna's art. Ethelbelle and Clayton became "family" and shared in the growth of the three boys and later their marriages and the joy of Edna and Tod's first granddaughter, Sami.

It was Edna, the artist, who caught the Craigs' attention with her beautiful paintings; but it was Edna, the woman, whose beautiful character drew the couple into a close relationship.

Shortly after they started collecting Hibels, Ethelbelle and Clayton went on a tour of France and visited the Renoir Museum in Cagnes. The building which houses the museum was the home of the famous artist before his death.

The Craigs went to Cagnes full of excitement, expecting to see a large exhibit of original Renoirs. They were shocked at the poor showing. The museum did not have a single original painting by the great French artist. Renoir's entire works had been sold and were in collections all over the world, most of them not even in France, the artist's homeland.

Ethelbelle and Clayton left France convinced of one thing: what happened to Renoir was not going to happen to Edna

Edna and Clayton Craig at the opening of the Hibel Museum

Hibel if they could help it. Until then they had been buying Hibels because they could not resist the personal pleasure they gained from the paintings. Now they began purchasing more and more of her work with a different goal in mind. That goal was not a secret. They were going to establish an Edna Hibel Museum so that years later when people visited the place where this American artist lived and worked they would find a worthy collection of originals waiting for them to enjoy.

While Mr. and Mrs. Craig were making plans for a permanent Hibel museum, they gave the public a chance to view and inevitably learn to appreciate their collection and Edna's paintings. Each canvas they bought was immediately hung someplace where people could see it. No part of the vast collection was ever put into storage. There was always a wall somewhere that needed a beautiful painting.

Starting in 1969, the Craig collection of Hibels went on tour to several U.S. cities on both the east and west coasts. Meanwhile, the couple continued to buy a growing number of Edna's paintings. By 1977 they had a total of one hundred and eighty paintings and over two hundred lithographs.

About this time, the Craigs received an invitation for a Hibel show at the National Museum of Fine Arts in Rio de Janiero, Brazil. A good part of the huge collection went out of the United States for the first time.

After the Rio de Janiero show, Mr. and Mrs. Craig began looking around seriously for the right place to establish the museum they planned to open for Edna. At last they found it. The building was in Palm Beach, Florida, a setting they thought was as lovely as the artist and woman they wanted to honor. After seventeen years of dreaming, and months of planning and work, on January 2, 1977, the Hibel Museum of Art opened to the public. A major portion of Edna Hibel's works of art were now settled and safe in their new home.

Edna stands outside the main entrance to the Museum

The museum Mr. and Mrs. Craig established made history. It is the first and only non-profit public foundation dedicated exclusively to the art of a living American woman artist. Both Craigs died shortly after the museum opened, but their interest in Edna Hibel as a woman and an artist has given the people of the United States a collection of original art everyone can be proud of today and in years to come.

The Hibel Museum of Art is "open to the public" as Edna herself has always been. It is a cultural center as well as a monument to the artist. One of the events it hosts is a series of "Promenade Concerts" performed by a wide range of musicians. The concerts began in 1979, when the directors and trustees decided that if visitors to the museum could listen to beautiful music while they viewed Edna's art, they would feel the artist's work more deeply. From the looks on the faces of those attending these events, that is exactly what is happening. Ethelbelle and Clayton Craig would be pleased.

Managing a Dual Career

Before Edna established herself as an artist, her life as a wife and mother was full to overflowing. Then Mabel Desmond came to live with the Plotkins and the household began to run like clockwork.

Mabel started to work for Tod and Edna in 1947 when Jonny was six years old. That same year, Andrew was born. A nurse came to help, but Mabel and Edna decided they could do better without her. The nurse stayed only one day.

"Mabel knew how to manage. That's the kind of person she was. She could always make do. She loved our children and they adored her. It was like having two mothers in the same house. She ran the place and us!" Edna laughs.

"Mabel had no family or children of her own, so we became her family. She was such a character, so competent and full of energy. We had many laughs together. Her friends would ask her, 'Mabel, how can you kiss those white children?' We both thought that was so funny.

"One day she overheard a friend of Andy's ask him, 'Is Mabel colored?' Andy shrugged his shoulders and said, 'I don't know.' That pleased Mabel as much as it pleased Tod and me."

"Mabel kept on top of everything and everyone," Edna recalls. "She was a wonderful cook. She prepared gourmet food long before that term became popular, and she insisted on a balanced diet. She was so proud of our family and her place in it. She made dinner a special occasion for all of us."

When the Plotkin family business failed, Edna had to tell Mabel that they could no longer afford her help.

"We both cried," Edna admits. "Mabel taught me how to cook and manage the household. Then she got a part-time job with a neighbor so she could keep an eye on us. That summer she insisted on coming to Hull with us. She was in such a happy mood, singing and laughing. We couldn't understand because it was a sad time for us. She confided in me that she had had a premonition that we were not going to lose everything. As it turned out, she was right. To us, it was almost a miracle. To Mabel, it was exactly what she expected.

"After we opened the gallery on Newbury Street in Boston, Mabel surprised us by deciding she wanted to run it while Lena was managing the gallery in Palm Beach. She did a wonderful job until she developed cataracts and had to undergo eye surgery."

Tod suggested that Mabel retire from work. She didn't need the money and she was getting up there in years.

"I'd die without the gallery!" Mabel objected.

She never left Boston. She did visit Florida with the Plotkins' granddaughter, Sami, one Christmas vacation and loved it, but she couldn't wait to get back to "her gallery."

Mabel was with Edna and Tod until she passed away in 1980. "She was my best friend, really," Edna says of Mabel. "None of us will ever forget her."

Certainly none of the Plotkin boys will ever forget Mabel, even though at the time they didn't realize how much her being there meant to Edna's career as an artist. How could they? They didn't even know she was an artist!

Andy's account of the moment he realized that his mother also had a professional life shows how well Edna was able to manage her dual career with Mabel's help, even with three young children underfoot:

> It never dawned on me that my mother was anything
> but the best mother in the whole wide world, you know,

your normal, average, everyday mother. I would come home from school every day, and she would come downstairs to find out how my day went and to serve me milk and cookies, my favorite snack. Sometimes my mom would then help me with a little homework, or cajole me into practicing my music, play a quiet game with me, or give me permission to play outside.

Then one day—I think I was twelve—she descended the stairs after I came home from school, and, after asking me how school was, she suggested I get a snack while she finished some work.

Several days of this 'Hi, honey, how was your day? You can get your own milk' piqued my curiosity. I was too embarrassed to find out from my mother what she was doing, so I inquired of my father.

He asked if I wanted to see. I nodded and he took me up the long, rambling stairs to the third floor attic, a place my younger brother, Dicky, and I were not encouraged to go because of the potential danger of a precipitous stairwell fall.

Entering into the largest of the three attic rooms, I saw paintings in progress on easels, and drawing pads strewn about. 'Your mother paints!' my father proudly pointed out.

'Wow' is all I could say several times. It all became clear to me then why she would always come bounding down the stairs to greet me. 'A painter,' I mused over and over again in my head. 'Wow.'

I asked what a pot was doing overflowing with white stuff as it sat in a corner on a single stove burner. My father patiently explained that my mother made her own gesso and plaster of paris to make frescoes, just like the painters did more than four hundred years ago. 'Wow.'

From then on, my mother didn't have to bound down two flights of stairs to greet me. Instead, I bounded up to see what was cooking!

Several years later, my parents built a studio onto the ground floor of the house, ostensibly to be able to provide air conditioning and more uncluttered space for my mother.

Mabel, at the opening of the Hibel Gallery on Newbury Street, Boston.

The first goal of cooling was accomplished, but the clutter only expanded to fill the additional space. Even at the unconscious age of nineteen I realized that such boundless energy and love as possessed my mother could never be contained into a well-defined space.

Frequently, Dicky and I would watch over my mom's shoulder as she painted at her easel. Occasionally, we would watch together. On one such occasion, she was holding a small oil painting on her lap as she neared its conclusion.

She poised a small paintbrush above her creation of an older woman sitting in her farmland somewhere in Europe, her hands folded benevolently on her lap. The brush came down with the tiniest dab of white paint to create a gnarled knuckle on the woman's thumb.

A lightning bolt might just as well have hit. Dicky and I both gasped. 'Did you see that?' he blurted out wide-eyed. 'Yeah, did you?' I sputtered back. 'Wow!' we both said in chorus, as my mother burst out laughing.

The painting sprang to life with that one stroke. The woman became immortalized it seemed, with one thunder-clap. My mother was so happy she could share with us such a magical moment so that Dicky and I could understand something about the creative process, and also understand the kind of exciting experiences that so often happened to her as she worked.

The Artist and the Woman Honored

As more people became familar with Edna's work, and art critics worldwide reviewed it favorably, her international reputation began to flourish. She was elected to the Royal Society of Art in London, England, and in 1976 was invited with Tod for a personal presentation to Queen Elizabeth II.

It was a prestigious occasion for an American artist and a new challenge for Edna. She admired the way the Queen handled her roles as wife, mother and national leader. She wondered what they would have to talk about, and if they would have a chance to talk person-to-person, woman-to-woman.

The big question in her family's mind was, "What will Edna wear?" Typically, Edna hadn't given it a thought. She never took fashion seriously. Even when the Plotkin family had their own department store, Edna only went shopping on rare occasions.

She liked wearing the same comfortable dresses she had worn many times before. When someone makes her buy a new outfit, she lets it hang in the closet a year or two to get used to it.

So what did Edna Hibel wear when she went to London to visit the Queen? She doesn't even remember! She is sure it was one of her old favorites. What she does remember is that Queen Elizabeth was easy to be with and friendly. There wasn't time for more than a few words because about thirty members of the royal family were presented to almost as many honored guests at the reception and banquet.

Edna directs a band in Dubrovnik, prior to the opening of her exhibit there.

It was also in 1976 that a milestone event took place in Edna's career. A small group of Hibel fans and collectors formed the Edna Hibel Society. Today there are ten thousand members from the United States, Canada, Europe and the Orient.

The Society publishes a newsletter to keep the members abreast of what is happening in Edna's life and career and to tell them about special art tours it sponsors. There are charter trips to such faraway places as Monte Carlo, Zurich, Dubrovnik and Beijing to attend the openings of major Hibel exhibits. One of the trips took them to Sweden, Norway, and Denmark where members mingled with royalty, governors, ambassadors and mayors as they toured the famous castles and museums where Edna's shows were held. Their sight-seeing ended with a flight to Helsinki and then to Leningrad for a real, Russian "red carpet" welcome.

In 1985, Society members travelled with Edna to Vienna, Austria for a "Celebration of Life" exhibit at the Galerie Palais Palffy. The show was held by invitation from the mayor of Vienna, Professor Doctor Helmut Zilk, a Hibel fan and admirer. The Vienna Festival was celebrated every five years, and on this occasion, Edna was the principal artist.

With the Society to help spread her fame, and with the newsletter faithfully published by Ralph Burg, President of the Edna Hibel Society, honors keep coming to Edna both for her art and for the woman behind the art. In 1982 she was named Humanitarian of the Year and given the Spirit of Life Award by the Palm Beach Chapter of the City of Hope. A few months later she received the Medal of Honor from the Netherlands Minister of Culture for her contribution to the arts, and a tribute from the Academia Flandriensis Pro Arte Scienciae et Letteras.

The following year there were a number of honors for Edna, among them the Medal of Honor and Citation from Pope John Paul II. Never before had the Vatican honored a woman artist, much less one of Jewish ancestry. Yet to Edna, it seemed perfectly natural.

"After all," she reasoned, "the Holy Family of Mary, Joseph and Jesus were Jewish. Besides, in the family of love there is no nationalism. Love makes us one human family."

Ralph Burg makes selections for an upcoming Edna Hibel Society Newsletter.

Edna says a few words at the United Nations reception.

Another meaningful event for Edna was the 1983 reception in her honor given by the United Nations in New York for her "Food for Peace" exhibit. This was a gala affair with all the United Nations ambassadors present. Members of the Edna Hibel Society were there, too. Edna created a "Mother Earth" painting for a limited art print as a United Nations first day cover for the World Federation. The cover is cacheted, which means it is on an envelope. The center design in delicate shades of blue, yellow and green is framed by Edna's hand-written words, "Mother Earth in the painting is symbolic of mothers in every corner of the world, feeding, nurturing, protecting — and of hopes and compassion." In November, 1986, a stamp with the same painting and inscription was issued and put on sale by the United States Postal Administration.

Still the honors kept coming. In March, 1984, Dr. Anthony T. Lodico, founder of the Academy of Collectible Art, announced that Edna had been named honoree of the year in two categories, "Best Artist of the Year: Collector Plates," and "Distinguished Humanitarian Award." Dr. Lodico said of Edna that she was chosen "in recognition of her well-known humanitarian efforts on behalf of children everywhere, and for her outstanding artistic achievements in the field of collectible art."

This honor was marked by the issue of the first Hibel Tribute plate, "Giselle," and the first Hibel Tribute poster, "Homage to all Children." Money from the sale of the plate was donated partly to the International Special Olympics and partly to the National Committee of Arts for the Handicapped. Both of these groups work with children in ways that touch Edna's heart. Her support touched their hearts, too. In May, 1985, Edna was invited to Columbia University as guest of honor at a reception given by Arts for the Handicapped. The best part, according to Edna, was being able to spend the day leading a group of "special" children between the ages of four and fourteen in an art workshop.

"It was a great thrill being with such children," she says of the experience. "They are so full of love and energy, and so eager to learn. I admit I learned as much as they did."

U.N. First Day cover

For her work with the Arts for the Handicapped, now known as Very Special Arts, Edna was accorded its Presidential Award—the first to anyone not a United States President—for her "vast humanitarian achievements spanning more than two decades."

Another honor Edna received in 1984 gave her a chance to share her talent with yet a different charitable organization, the Little Flower Society of the Order of the Carmelites. Father Terrence L. Sempowski tells how this came about.

"I was passing an art gallery while walking downtown in Chicago when my eye caught a striking picture of a mother and child. It was so beautiful that I had to go into the gallery and ask who painted it.

"The clerk told me it was a Hibel and mentioned that the artist, Edna Hibel, would be at the gallery in a few weeks for a reception. I bought a book of her paintings and lithographs, took it home, and fell in love with her work.

"When I went back to the gallery for the reception, it overflowed with people. I ended up in a long line, book in hand. I wanted Edna to sign the book, but I also wanted to ask if she might do a painting for a Christmas card for our Little Flower Society. By the time I made it to the front of the line, I came to the conclusion that Edna Hibel was a much more famous artist than I had realized."

That fact made Father Terry nervous.

"Then when Edna looked up and smiled at me, I relaxed totally. She was looking at me as if I were her best friend in the whole world. After having her autograph my book, I told her about the Society and asked if she would be interested in painting a Christmas card for us.

"Her warm expression didn't change, but she said she never accepted commissions to do paintings. Then she hesitated

Edna and Dr. Oscar Arias, President of Costa Rica

and said, 'This isn't really a good time to talk to me now, Father Terry. Why don't you get in touch with me at home?'

"I fell in love with her art, but it was puppy love compared with what I felt when I finally had the chance to get to know Edna herself. Someone has said that Edna Hibel radiates love and warmth 'like a grandmother fresh from cookie-baking.' She glows, bubbles, smiles, and laughs. Her dark eyes, which see so much kindness and beauty in people, are sparkling and magnetic. They capture you."

Father Terry and Edna discovered they had the same views of life. They became close friends, and Edna contributed the first of a series of Christmas cards for the Little Flower Society. Their sale continues to be a success.

For Father Terry, his meeting with Edna Hibel, woman and artist, was more than a human coincidence. It was more than two people from such different religions, social and ethnic backgrounds, who just happened to come together by accident. He wrote later, "A coincidence is a miracle in which God prefers to remain anonymous."

In 1988, Edna received two honorary doctorate degrees in arts and letters. In February, the University for Peace in Costa Rica, chartered by the United Nations, presented Edna the degree "For her contribution to peace through art which captures the beauty of Humanity and Nobility and Dignity with which people bear their burdens." In May, Edna received her second doctorate from Mount Saint Mary's College in Maryland, the oldest Catholic seminary in the United States. For this occasion Edna and Tod were invited to stay at the campus "White House." Usually reserved for high church officials, this home/museum originally belonged to Elizabeth Ann Seton, the first saint from America, as recognized by the Catholic Church. President Robert J. Wickenheiser presented the diploma to Edna stating, "... these recognitions have not only been for your work as an artist, but as a great humanitarian, who sees the world with beautiful eyes. ..."

Hibel in China

Two very special events in Edna Hibel's career took place in 1986. She was elected to a Fellowship in the World Academy of Art and Science (WAAS), and then she received an invitation from the People's Republic of China to be the first foreign woman artist to exhibit her paintings in that country.

Edna considers the Fellowship in the World Academy of Art and Science to be one of the most prestigious and unexpected things that has happened in her career.

WAAS is an association which includes forty-three Nobel Laureates. Its focus is transcultural, transdisciplinary and transnational. Membership is limited to no more than five hundred individuals chosen for eminence in art, natural and social sciences, and the humanities. It functions "as an informal 'world university' at the highest scientific and ethical level, in which deep human understanding and the fullest sense of responsibility meet." Edna Hibel, upon being made a Fellow, was the very first painter so honored. The only other artist included in WAAS was Henry Moore, the noted late English sculptor.

Then in September of 1986 Edna led her history-making trip to China. It had taken five years for the official China Exhibition Agency to arrange for this event. It all began when Edna met a Hibel fan from Toronto, Canada at a dinner party. The man introduced himself as "Charlie Chaplin."

"And I'm Cleopatra!" Edna laughed, sure that he was joking.

That unusual introduction was the start of another close friendship. The man's real name was indeed Charlie Chaplin. He knew the Chinese Ambassador to Canada, and after seeing Edna's paintings and meeting her, he suggested the idea of a Hibel exhibit in China.

A short time later, Madame Ge Qiyon, wife of the Chinese Ambassador to the United States, gave a talk at the Hibel Museum of Art for the US–China Peoples Friendship Association. She felt a strong bond with Edna's paintings, as did her husband, the Honorable Han Xu. They were sure that Edna's art would be well received by the Chinese people.

And it was. On one day, twenty-thousand visitors came to see "The World I Love," the Hibel exhibit at the China National Art Gallery in Beijing. Over one hundred million Chinese saw the opening ceremonies on China's televised evening news program. Here is what the news reporter said:

Edna sketches the Temple of Heaven in Beijing.

"Fifty-three oil paintings displayed how Edna Hibel loves life, people and painting. The subjects of the art works are wide-ranging. Her colors are so really warm with discovered richness. Her paintings much affected all the spectators, especially the paintings of mother and children which she produced so tender, beautiful and lovingly that they made Edna wring the hearts of the Chinese people."

Besides the television story, Beijing Radio broadcast an interview with Edna heard by millions of Chinese people. There were interviews and articles in the *People's Daily* and other Chinese newspapers and magazines. According to the editor of the *Chinese Literature Magazine*, "some people may well sell their bicycles to raise funds for travel expenses to visit the exhibit."

Edna said that after seeing how many bicycles there were in China, three million in the heart of Beijing alone, she realized the sacrifice "selling their wheels" represented in that country. Yet whole families, some of them travelling great distances, came to see the Hibel exhibit during the two weeks it was in Beijing.

While she was in China, Edna was asked to lead a workshop for advanced students at the Central Institute of Fine Arts. She used one of the students as a model. The class was so interested in her work that Edna left them her supply of paints, some of which are not available in China.

Edna was allowed to visit a commune where people were as excited about her visit as she was to be there. They took pictures of her with nursery school children and teachers. Edna remembers them as "beautiful people. I will never forget them."

From Beijing, "The World I Love" exhibit went to the Sichuan Institute of Fine Art in Chongqing, formerly Chungking, a city of ten million people. The two-week stay was a huge success with thousands of people going to view it.

Students are very attentive as Edna demonstrates at the Beijing Art Institute.

One of the things Edna wanted to do in China was to find her good friend and classmate, Winnie Cheng. Winnie and Edna had studied together at the Boston Museum School of Fine Arts. Winnie posed for a large canvas in 1939 which Edna called "Portrait of Winnie Cheng." The portrait was sold and later purchased by a friend and given to the Hibel Museum. It is the earliest of the fifty-three paintings included in "The World I Love" exhibit.

"Winnie was a lovely individual with a lovely face," Edna says of her friend. "We had a lot of good times together. Then I left Boston to paint in Mexico and Winnie returned to China. She married Professor Huang of the Shanghai University. I heard from her a few times after that and knew she had a child.

We lost track of each other, so when I knew I was going to China I hoped and prayed I could find Winnie again."

Edna had everyone looking for her lost friend in China. She talked about Winnie when she was interviewed and posed in front of the portrait so the picture would be published. Still, she found out nothing. She was very disappointed.

"Then several months after I came home," Edna continues, "I received a letter from Winnie's youngest son, Henry. It was from Maryland, USA. A relative in China sent Henry a copy of a magazine story telling about my search for Winnie. He looked up my address in *Who's Who in American Art* and wrote the letter. It was wonderful hearing from Winnie's son, even though he had sad news about his mother."

Edna learned that Winnie and her husband had been put in prison during the Cultural Revolution in China. They were badly treated and died shortly after being released. Their three sons, however, were able to come to the United States. Edna couldn't wait to meet Henry and his two older brothers. It was like having part of Winnie back again.

Edna herself chose each of the paintings included in the exhibit that went to China. She wanted "to give the viewers a feeling for the full scope of . . . all the subjects I love."

Here is one of the letters to Edna that shows her message was received:

Dear Edna,

We always precious your friendship, and your love and care not only make us happy, so much meaning to be able to help and love each other. But most important fulfill part of our life. We sincerely thank you for such a lovely person. We all love you. Please take care!

Love,
Daniel Hsu

Portrait of Winnie Cheng, oil on canvas, 50" x 32"

Vice President George Bush called Edna's 1986 trip to China "a cultural exchange and a worthwhile contribution to improving United States/China relations."

More than ninety members of the Edna Hibel Society followed Edna to China to help with the "red" ribbon cutting ceremonies at the National Museum.

"The Chinese people are so graceful—even while eating, which is so rarely graceful."
—Edna

Upward and Onward

With a museum dedicated to her work, and with the Edna Hibel Society and her family to back her, Edna is still reaching out to touch people. In each medium she uses, Edna strikes a special chord with her admirers. From her paintings and lithographs, to her collector plates and clay sculptures, Edna communicates her values through her various forms of self-expression.

Her doll collection provides a good example of this. Edna began making cloth dolls for friends as a child and later, as a mother, for her own children. Today, her exquisite porcelain dolls are winning the highest awards.

"I create a doll the way I create any work of art, with an image and a burst of ecstatic energy," she admits. Then she adds, "I love working in porcelain. The translucency is perfect for the faces. Every minute is a new discovery."

It didn't take Edna long to discover that dressing the dolls was as much fun as creating their faces. The fabrics she uses come from all over the world and complement each doll's personality. Her collection of originals includes many series, the latest called "Rosalie."

Creating these dolls and seeing the pleasure they bring to people of all ages is not enough for Edna. Once a year, she presides over a Doll Festival and Tea Party held in the Hibel Museum. The day is complete with refreshments served on the lawns overlooking the Intracoastal Waterway. Guests come great distances to spend the afternoon with Edna, to have their Hibel dolls autographed, and to witness the mold-breaking ceremony for that year's creation.

Edna, working on a doll in her studio

Granddaughter Wendy, holding the Wendy Doll.

No one was surprised when Edna's fascination with porcelain led her to try her hand at ornaments and miniatures as well. She uses her finest brushes and pale pastel colors to do the faces and figures of mothers and children on the hard-paste medallions which measure only one to three inches across. In these mediums, Hibel admirers with smaller incomes can afford to own a Hibel, which pleases Edna immensely. "Art has to be affordable," she insists.

Meanwhile, with Tod at her side, Edna is travelling more widely than ever. Through her one-artist shows and exhibits, the Hibel name now crosses the Atlantic and Pacific oceans as easily as her brush strokes skim across canvas.

To date, she has had well over one hundred shows, some of them in the most beautiful cities, castles, universities, museums, and art galleries in the world.

Not all of the cities she has visited are tranquil. Her one-artist show in Jerusalem took place in an ancient site steeped in history and religious struggle. People from many

Tod pulls all of the art supplies

A crowd gathers around Edna as she paints in Rhodes.

cultural backgrounds came to view her paintings at the Hebrew University there. The Hibel message of love, peace, and beauty brought hope to families in a land torn by troubles. In the Holy Land, she recognized the same glow of youth and the same wisdom of age that had sparked her artistic talent when she visited the rural Amish or the Seminole Indians in the United States. The images she carried back to her studio from Jerusalem have resulted in some of her greatest paintings.

Very recently, when Edna returned to Israel, she made another of her surprising discoveries: original multi-colored serigraphs, a type of silk screen printing.

During a brief tour of the Ezra Sultan silk screen printing studio in Tel Aviv, Edna acquainted herself with three presses, sixteen drying racks, screen processing procedures, and the back-lit drawing tables, all necessary to the process. Then, Edna went to work. For her and for the shop technicians, that meant a week of intense effort. Everyone was exhausted but Edna. She was too excited with the results to feel anything but elation. Here was another medium for her artistic expression.

Of all the countries where Edna has had exhibits in recent years, no two bring more bittersweet memories than the former Yugoslavia and the former Soviet Union. She is saddened by the turmoil and destruction that are hurting so many people she came to love while visiting there.

This is particularly true in Yugoslavia where her exhibit in Dubrovnik, the loveliest of cities, was hailed by a resident as "the best event we've had in one hundred years." National feelings were so strong that foreign artists had rarely been permitted to have shows in that country, and never before was the work of a foreign woman shown. Miles of red tape were patiently untangled before the Hibel exhibit was approved.

Edna's show broke the museum's record for an opening night. More than thirty-five hundred visitors came to see forty pieces of her pioneering work in oil glaze and gold-leaf paintings. National barriers fell immediately. The people of Yugoslavia invited Edna to stay as long as she wanted. She was able to extend the show only five days before having to leave what Edna describes as "the most beautiful city with the most beautiful people." Now the city has been diminished and many lives lost. Edna's work has since been used to benefit refugees of the wars in the former Yugoslavia, and she hopes someday her work will help inspire the restoration of Dubrovnik.

Her June, 1990 trip to the Soviet Union to exhibit at the Museum of the Soviet Union Academy of Art and at the Exhibition Hall of the Russian Union of Artists in Leningrad made her the only foreigner ever invited to hold more than one exhibit in that country. As in Yugoslavia and China, she was also the first foreign woman artist allowed to exhibit in the Soviet Union.

In addition to these two "firsts," Edna worked for nearly a month to make a one-hour television documentary. Produced as a joint venture, "Hibel's Russian Palette" is the only television production created by a foreign woman in the former Soviet Union.

The documentary, as reported in the Edna Hibel Society's Newsletter, "allowed the seventy-three year old artist and grandmother of five the opportunity to be among the first international visitors to hold intimate, in-depth conversations with laborers, students, artists, government officials, church officials,

The crowds in Dubrovnik set a record for attendance at an art exhibit.

professionals, farmers, fishermen, refuseniks, and other Soviet citizens in their apartments, work places, and religious institutions, as well as in the streets, subways, and market places of Yalta, Novgorod, Leningrad, Moscow, and Zagorsky."

"Originally, I just wanted to meet a few people, see some of Russia's famous museums and cultural events," Edna explains, "and indeed I was able to view many cultural sights and create paintings, drawings, lithographs, and porcelain art. But *glasnost* and *perestroika* were in full swing," she continues, "and my wonderful Russian guides and television crew offered to give me a real inside look at what was actually happening in the Soviet Union. Now that was an offer I couldn't refuse!"

Once again, Edna touched those she worked with on the project. Nikolai, a rugged Soviet cameraman, wept openly as Edna boarded the airplane to leave. Millions of Americans will also be touched by the broadcast of this historic program in 1994.

One of the most memorable moments of her Soviet experience was at the Museum of the Soviet Academy of Art. While touring the museum, she saw a group of paintings by Alexander Yacovlev, her former teacher at the Boston Museum School of Fine Arts. It was as if her professional career had come full circle. The memory of her beloved Yacovlev brought tears of joy to her eyes.

Her appeal in the international arena just goes on. Two very special events are scheduled for 1994. Boys' Town of Italy will be bestowing upon Edna its International Humanitarian of the Year Award, a rare honor. The award is given infrequently, not annually as its name suggests. The only other two recipients in the past decade have been Perry Como and Joe DiMaggio.

In so honoring Edna, those making the award went beyond the population of Italian descent to someone of Jewish background.

Edna's international recognition continues to grow in Asia as well as in Europe. In April of 1994, she will have the distinct honor of presenting an exhibit of her work at the prestigious Mitsukoshi Department Store in Tokyo. Indeed, it seems that all the world loves both Edna and her artwork.

Family in and of the 1990s

While Edna the artist still puts in fourteen hours a day to keep up the flow of her creative ideas, Edna the woman continues to put family first. She and Tod continue to work on projects together and to share their love of the arts and of each other.

Jon Plotkin (Jonny), now fifty-two, has a private environmental consulting firm in the Palm Beaches. He also directs the murder mystery plays that his wife, Gail, writes and produces. His ties with his childhood bring him back to the Boston area during the summer where he is a commercial lobster fisherman. He also does commercial fishing in the Palm Beaches during the winter. When called upon, Jon takes photographs for Edna Hibel Studio events and hangs the new exhibitions at the Hibel Museum of Art. Jon and Gail's daughter, Sami, is also involved in the arts as a filmmaker.

Andrew Plotkin (Andy), now forty-six, is the vice president of Edna Hibel Studio (also known as Edna Hibel Corp.) He serves as special liaison with the Edna Hibel Society, helps direct the Edna Hibel Gallery, is the executive trustee of the Hibel Museum of Art, and directs all international affairs for Edna Hibel. Occasionally, he still plays tennis, and sings in choruses and quartets specializing in a capella barbershop harmony. Andy's wife, Cheryll, is the financial manager of Edna Hibel Studio, Edna Hibel Gallery, and the Hibel Museum of Art. Their children are Wendy and Joshua.

Richard Plotkin (Dicky), now forty-three, directs Richard's Gallery in Hyannis, Massachusetts, and manages real estate in the Boston area. He sang for several years with brother Andy

Andy and Cheryll Plotkin

Toddy, Edna and Dicky

Jennie, Edna and Tod

in a barbershop quartet, and was an active musician in Boston for a number of years. Dicky has two children, Jennie and Toddy.

Among Edna's loving and admiring relatives, her daughter-in-law Gail, Jonny's wife, has expressed some beautiful and especially apt thoughts about her:

> I have often said, and truly believe, that if Edna had never painted a single picture she'd still be the most extraordinary woman I've ever met.
>
> We lived together for many summers in a big old wooden house on the ocean in Hull, Massachusetts. The house was a former hotel complete with telephone booth and a big silver cash register. My husband Jon, Edna's eldest son, had a large organic garden in the backyard. Edna painted in two large rooms on the second floor. I wrote in a room on the third floor and Tod on the second just below me. My daughter Sami had a room in our section as well as one in Edna and Tod's. Edna's sons, Richard and Andrew, came on weekends with their wives.
>
> It was a magic time. Jon's fresh lobsters and vegetables. The ocean at our door. And Edna. I found her once long after dark on her hands and knees doing something in the backyard. "You said you loved English gardens so I'm making you one," she said. And she had. So many tiny stones lining little paths going nowhere, but definitely English.
>
> And then of course there were the flowers. I'd see Edna outside early in the morning in her paint-stained pants and shirt working away with her spade and trowel. Thanks to Edna, flowers bordered the entire house. Once we had a whole boat full of poppies. Another time I told her how much I loved Roses of Sharon and she surprised me with a tree. Most of all, Edna loves wild flowers. We'd go out into the fields to pick them and then hurry home so she could paint them. Queen Ann's Lace never had it so good.

Jonny and Gail Plotkin

Those summers were very special to our daughter Sami. She really had four parents. All over the house were projects that one or all of us were doing with her.

At three Sami was diagnosed with lazy eye. Most of the time she was supposed to wear a patch over her good eye to strengthen the weak one. Edna taped over the lens of one side of her glasses and painted a rose on it. It somehow made the wearing of the eye covering more palatable. Then Edna found the tiniest of playing cards and for hours played all kinds of card games with Sami. Just recently Sami, who is now twenty-seven, said to me, "Isn't it funny how grandma used to love to play cards with me?" She never knew.

That's one of the nicest things about Edna. She always takes a positive view. For instance, I first met her when Jon invited me for a weekend to their beach house. Just before dinner Edna asked me to set the table. I told her I didn't know how. In my house we never sat down to a meal together. Edna said, "Wonderful, I can teach you." Not, "How could you be nineteen years old and not know how to set a table?" So she taught me. She also taught me how to park a car. I had my license but still couldn't really park. I suppose the favorite thing she taught me was flower arranging. I had never thought of myself as someone who could do anything with my hands.

If I had to say what it is about Edna that gives her that certain something exceptional, it would be her total acceptance of whoever she meets. I've seen the worst sort of people behave like angels on encountering her. With Edna you feel liked, even admired. I've often said, she can charm the birds off the trees.

When I first knew Edna I thought she was perfect. Then about ten years into our relationship I realized she is human, and after a while I forgave her for it. I don't think these were conscious thoughts. I understand them looking back.

What Edna did for me, besides giving me her firstborn and showering me with Hibels, was just to be Edna. The best way to teach is by example. I learned it's not what happens to one in life but how one copes and goes on. Edna and Tod don't waste one precious moment complaining. They see what is and do what has to be done.

When someone feels this way about her mother-in-law, what more is there to say?

Sami, Wendy, and Joshua Plotkin

Faith and Art

What part has faith played in the life and career of Edna Hibel?

If her works of art say anything, they say that Edna's faith in goodness and love was and is a big part of her success. Whether she was born with that faith or it sprang from a happy home and childhood, she definitely has it. A lot of it.

Edna's Jewish background gives strength to her belief in God, in a divine power that loves, guides and governs. She believes in mankind, in humanity, in the beautiful things that happen to people who love and respect each other. She believes in herself, not above others, but equal to any other human being.

Edna Hibel's faith is not denominational. It is something she shares easily and naturally with everyone regardless of race, creed or nationality. Her faith does not divide people or goodness into groups, nor does it pit and compare one against the other. Edna thinks, lives, and paints in terms of togetherness. Her favorite themes are mothers and children and family togetherness.

A quick study of her vast work shows there is not one negative painting in all the thousands she has completed since her first drawing in the fourth grade in Allston, Massachusetts. Most are of women and children in many combinations or of children alone and in groups. Some are of people working on their farms in faraway places and people of all ages being themselves. Other paintings are still lifes, florals, landscapes, cityscapes, and seascapes. A few of the faces Edna draws are

Tod and Edna on a recent trip

tired or careworn, but there is no anger, hate, resentment, revenge, jealousy, or any unkind image in her paintings.

Those who know Edna best say there are no unkind images in the Hibel art because there are none in the artist herself. Deep feelings are there, hopes and fears, but nothing that pulls people apart or destroys human togetherness. Her art, like her mind, celebrates the world as really good and beautiful and depicts human kind as a proud achievement.

We asked the artist to tell us how she has been able to keep her faith in goodness, in the power of love, so strong when there is so much wrongdoing in the world. Here is part of what she had to say:

"Perhaps it is *because* so much is made of the hate and ugliness in the world that I appreciate the love and beauty I see and feel. I have been fortunate to have been given eyes that see light instead of darkness.

"Right in the middle of the awful things that make the headlines, there is human tenderness, joy, warm feelings toward others, and love. I can find it in the look on a child's face, in the exquisite forms on nature's growing things. Even a small thing like a blade of grass has its own special color and beauty. So does each flower, no matter how humble the place where it takes root. So does each changing view of the sky, of mountains and fields no matter which country or national boundary lays claim to it.

"I have to believe that we can look to our young people with hope that they will make the world live up to nature's fantastic possibilities. I don't think hope is useless. I think it is what clears our vision so we can see the beauty of goodness in all people and all things.

"How can I *not* keep the faith as long as there are children and the glad promise they hold in their hands?

"Art is my way of being true to that faith. To me, it is just being Edna Hibel."

Artwork

Index

About the Author

Olga Cossi is the author of a number of books for children. Her book, *The Magic Box*, was selected for the New York Public Library's "Books for the Teen Age" list, and *Harp Seals* was named "the most outstanding children's science trade book" by the Children's Book Council and the National Science Teachers Association.

Of her writing she says, "I am a word weaver. Words are music to me. I love to weave stories with them, to see the look on someone's face when they are touched by what I have written.

"My biography of Edna Hibel is a story whose time has come. Her life will touch readers of all ages."